Spaghetti Dinner

A history of spaghetti eating and cooking for:

Spaghetti Dinner

by

GIUSEPPE PREZZOLINI

COACHWHIP PUBLICATIONS
Greenville, Ohio

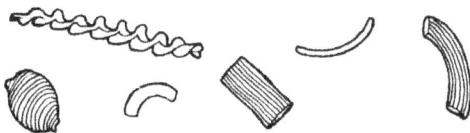

Spaghetti Dinner, by Giuseppe Prezzolini
© 2018 Coachwhip Publications

Giuseppe Prezzolini (1882-1982)
Published 1955.
No claims made on public domain material.

CoachwhipBooks.com

ISBN 1-61646-448-8
ISBN-13 978-1-61646-448-6

Table of Contents

List of Illustrations

To my friend
Giovanni Buitoni
who has the world's oldest factory of macaroni products

Spaghetti Dinner

Introduction
1

"To spy you
To try you
Proves you're the dish for me!
Then watch me eat
Until replete
I faint in ecstasy!"

—SGRUTTENDIO.°

Traveling the broad highways that cut across this country, no one can fail to note the number of times one particular invitation is extended to the American people. It shines forth at night in luminous neon signs. By day it is blazoned on brightly colored posters. It appears on the truckman's diner and the exclusive road-house. It is an invitation to lunch . . . to dinner . . . to a between-meals snack. It is a call to a dish which has fast been moving into position as one of America's most popular eating pleasures—the "Spaghetti Dinner."

Probably few of the restaurant owners who place that sign in their windows or on the walls of their diners know or care about the real meaning of the Italian word *spago*, which literally means "string." But they all know that spaghetti—"little strings"—is an Italian word. Its increasing use, as a word and as a food, represents a cultural gift from Italy to America. In this country the language of Dante may have been drowned out by Italian-American jargon, but spaghetti is well-known throughout the land,

°Filippo Sgruttendio, *La Collezione di tutti i poemi in lingua napoletana*, Tiorba a taccone, Napoli, Porcelli, 1783-89, vol. I. Sgruttendio is a famed Neapolitan poet, details of whose life are unknown.

1

in homes where the name of Dante is never pronounced. It is an expression of the collective genius of the Italian people and, in spaghetti, the Italian spirit has survived virtually intact.

Spaghetti is an Italian word, but *dinner* has been English for a long time. *Spaghetti dinner* is, then, a coined phrase, a marriage certificate between two countries, expressing a unity—half Italian, half English—and all American.

But what is it, this spaghetti? Where was it created? Who was the inventor?

There are an enormous number of stories about the invention of spaghetti and, unfortunately, they all appear to be inventions themselves. In those primordial days when the first "little strings" made their appearance there were certainly no historians around to record the event. So the myth-makers of all nations got busy. Still today the Chinese, the Japanese, the Germans, the French, and the Italians from the top to the toe of the boot, fight for the crown of discoverer. Each section of Italy makes use of every saying, phrase, legend, memory or tradition to press its claim. You hear "positive proof" from the Neapolitans, from the Sicilians, and from the boys from Cagliari. But when any of these claims is investigated at close range, it fails to stand up.

Oddly the most widely accepted legend is the most dubious of the lot. According to this legend it was Marco Polo who, on his journey through China, saw spaghetti being made there and brought it back to Venice, where it speedily gained favor and became Italy's national dish. This tale with an infinite number of colorful variations°

———
°One recent version is titled *A Legend of Love:*
"One day, hundreds of years ago, a young Chinese maiden was busy preparing her daily batch of bread dough. Becoming en-

has so well established its place in spaghetti lore that it usually appears unquestioned in the most scholarly cookbooks and compendiums of culinary history. The trouble is it is just not true. Marco Polo lived from 1254 to 1323 A.D. But already by the year 1200 the food was well enough known in Italy to be mentioned in an historical document. The document is the *Life of the Blessed Hermit William°* and in it the following sentence occurs: "He invited William to dinner, and served macaroni." Presumably William was invited to a real dinner with real macaroni. So the food must have been in Italy at least a century before Marco Polo, according to the legend, introduced it to the country.

Moreover, in his book Marco Polo never refers to either spaghetti or macaroni. In the edition of his work published by Ramusio in 1559 and today not considered reliable, he does mention having seen the Chinese produce strips of dough he calls *lasagne*. But *lasagne,* and in general all forms of dough made from wheat and then dried in the sun, were well known in Italy long before the time of Marco Polo. And, significantly, when he saw these strips he recognized them and called them by a name from his own Venetian dialect. He did not use a Chinese word

---

grossed in conversation with an ardent Italian sailor, she forgot her task. Presently dough overflowed from the pan and dripped in strings that quickly dried in the sun. When he observed what had happened, the young Italian, hoping to hide the evidence of his loved one's carelessness, gathered the strings of dried dough and took them to his ship. The ship's cook boiled them in a broth. He was pleased to find that the dish was appetizing and savory. Upon the ship's return to Italy, word of the delicious new dish spread rapidly, and soon it was popular throughout the land."
—NATIONAL MACARONI INSTITUTE

°Dominus Du Cange, *Glossarium Mediae et Infimae Latinitatis,* Tomus V (Maccarones) p. 159, Paris, 1938. Acta B. Guillelmi Eremit. tom. I, Aprilis p. 383.

for them as he would have done had the product been unknown to him. The word *lasagne* has a long history but none of it connects with Chinese culture. It is a product of the Mediterranean civilization, from the Greek *lasanon* (or tripod) and the Latin *lasanum* (or saucepan).

No. This most widely accepted legend stands up no better than the others.

One addition to it which has been circulated in millions of copies of a prominent cookbook is remarkable for its extravagant inaccuracy. After repeating the story that the food came from China, the book tells us that "It had become so popular by the thirteenth century that Emperor Frederick II coined the word *macaroni* from *marcus* meaning *divine dish*."[*]

It is hard to say which part of this statement is the most amazing: the idea that even a "divine dish" could become widely popular without having a name attached to it, the idea that Frederick II "coined" a word which was already in use, or the idea that Frederick II coined his word from the word *marcus*. *Marcus* is not a word meaning anything in any language with which Emperor Frederick II was familiar, if it exists in any language.

It is possible that a printing error made *marcus* out of the Greek word *makarios*. *Makarios* does mean blessed, or fortunate, but only when used in reference to the dead, presumably in the sense that when you're dead you're better off. *Makarios* is related to the word *makaria*, food eaten in honor of the dead. The story, then, has perhaps an element of truth in it. The word *macaroni* probably comes from *makaria*, the name for food served at funeral banquets. But this word, like most others used in the macaroni-making art, is entirely Mediterranean, in this case

[*]*Betty Crocker's Picture Cook Book* (General Mills), New York, McGraw-Hill, 1950.

Greek. This indicates, if it does not prove, something about the origin of the food. Certainly if it had emerged from another section of the world, we would find Nordic, or Oriental, or some other linguistic roots in technical words—such as we find in the art of medieval seamanship.

This is about as far as scholarship takes us in establishing the ultimate source of the divine dish. However, we can enjoy our spaghetti dinner even without knowing whether it was first served at a Roman banquet or in a Chinese pagoda.

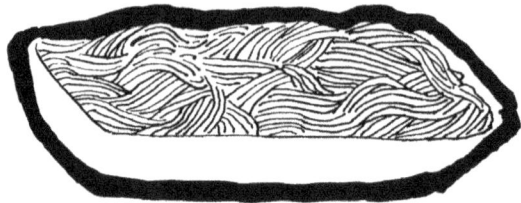

2

"From this dough you get the little bows,
The spiral fanfares and the star-dust,
The organ pipes and the furbelows,
The roller coasters and the pie crust."
         —free translation from ANTONIO VIVIANI.[*]

Although the origin of spaghetti cannot be pinned down
with great exactitude, it is certain that today, as for cen-
turies, it is identified primarily with the Mediterranean and
with Italy in particular. Almost every country in the world
knows how to mix flour and water and make bread. But
the fantastic and varied shapes of *pasta* in the macaroni
family—of which spaghetti is only one—owe their origin
to the imagination of the Italian people. Only a people
gifted with great fantasy, and accustomed to meeting fantasy daily, could have found so many forms—and names
for the forms—for this commonest of their foods. They
found forms and names in every aspect of their daily

[*]Antonio Viviani, *Li Maccheroni di Napoli*, poemetto giocoso di
Antonio Viviani, Napoli, Nella Stamperia della Società Filomatica,
1824, pp. viii, 48.

6

lives—in the earth, the sky, the sea, the professions, clothing, customs, historical events.

In the more than one hundred and fifty varieties of macaroni products you would search a long time to find a prosaic name. One unimaginative American, commenting that it was all dough, once suggested that the best way to distinguish between varieties would be to number them; "Give me a pound of macaroni Number 15."

For this lack of imagination the average American has been rewarded with a punishment to fit his crime. He has inherited few types of macaroni. He knows spaghetti, of course; probably vermicelli and noodles (a German dish brought to America by the German immigrants some fifty years before the Italians came over in full force). But aside from these, and maybe in more recent years *ravioli* and *lasagne*, there is no great variety of macaroni products to be found in the average American home.

Not so in Italy! Little pipes, butterflies, needle points, stars and turbans rub elbows with rings, little worms and tempests. The Italians couldn't possibly give cold, unfeeling numbers or simple descriptive names to macaroni, because the macaroni family is their own—a vital companion in their world. And the Italian world is cordial and convivial. It is colored and enriched with a wealth of terms—graceful diminutives, gay superlatives, marvelous exaggerations. Some macaroni names are really nicknames, signs of the same tender affection which inspires parents whimsically to shorten or modify their children's names. Have you ever eaten "eensy-weensy cannon"? Or "itsy-bitsy shells"? The Italians have!

You name it—the Italians have it! One type of macaroni is called pens and a type of pen which has been cut at an angle is called badly cut. Sometimes the same shape has a different name, according to the region in Italy in which it is made. One type is called little cuts

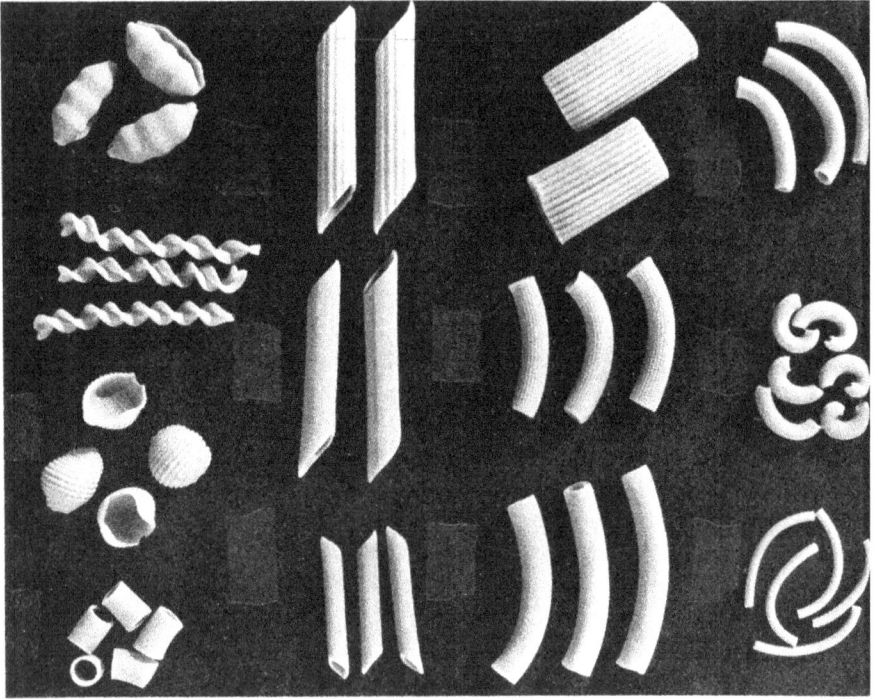

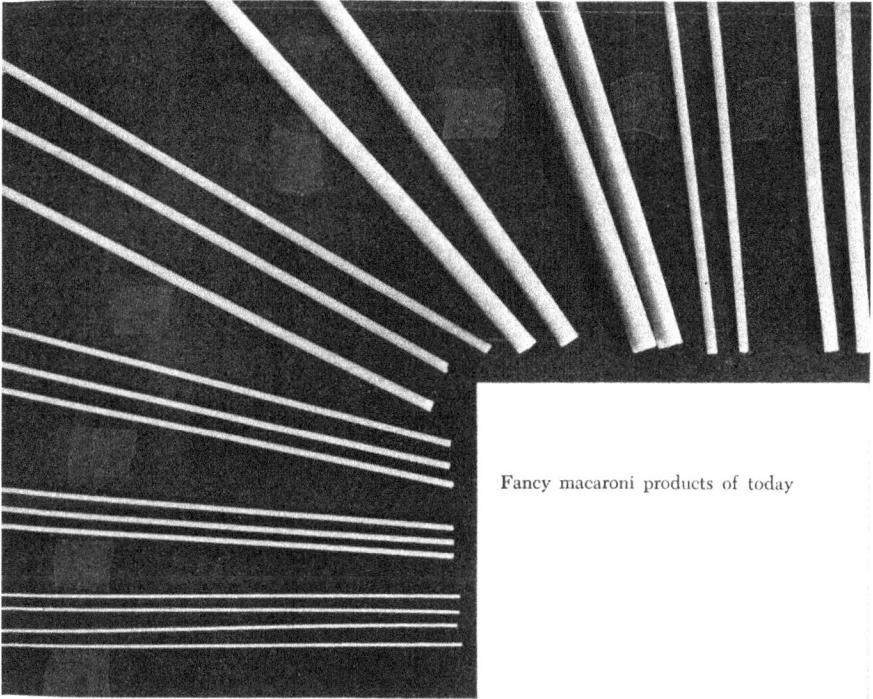

Fancy macaroni products of today

in Bologna, and little slices in Rome. Although such different names symbolize regional divisions in Italy, they also denote an overall unity of the peninsula, since it is the same macaroni shapes which, wandering here and there, become diffused—and confused with each other.

Since the Italian imagination is a naturalistic and unrestrained one, and Italians are pretty frank in their conversation, you might expect to run across some macaroni names which are suggestive. This is rare. There is, however, one macaroni named lady's legs and one called greedy priests. This last reflects the anti-clerical feeling which has been evident in so much of Italian literature. As a rule the Italians have been discreet in naming their macaronis —without taking all the fun out of life.

The Italian love of musical sound also pervades their macaroni-making. They have named one type of macaroni "clover" because, as it slides from the package into the pot, it makes a peculiar rustling sound similar to that made by dried clover as it falls into barn-yard feed bins.

"The really fine macaroni maker is a musician," writes Giovanni Comisso, one of contemporary Italy's most sensitive writers. "Every variation of the shorter cuts of macaroni has a different sound at just the right moment. All are sounds which match the notes in a musical scale. The least change in humidity will change the note. So will unwise handling. Then, like an instrument that's out of tune, the whole harmony is changed."°

Perhaps some day macaroni will inspire a modern composer, as some of our finest composers have been inspired by a stage coach, the sound of a cuckoo, and the harmonies of the pines of Rome.

°Giovanni Comisso, article in *Il Tempo*, 27 November 1949: "Potenza della Gastronomia per l'unità dei popoli—Dimmi quel che mangi e ti dirò chi sei."

Another thing that has always fascinated Italians has been the eyes of animals. They are impressed by their roundness, their luminosity, their minuteness. The tiny eyes

Giovanni Comisso (b. 1895)

are reproduced in the little macaroni dots that appear in broth. The machine that makes these is going to perfect itself right out of existence; the dots are getting progressively more minuscule until, one day, like the grin of the Cheshire Cat, or like old soldiers, they may just fade away.

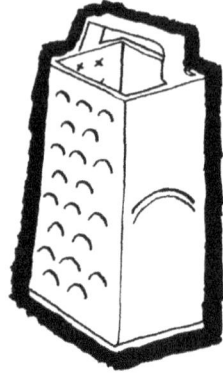

3

*"All an Eighteenth Century poet,
French or Russian, had to do to
make his poem authentically Italian
was to rhyme 'lazzaroni' with
'macaroni.'"*
    —Antonio Baldini.°

Small wonder that the Italians have this enormous affection for macaroni, for they have grown up with it, literally and figuratively. One of the first Italian historians was a Franciscan monk, Fra Salimbene of Parma. In a chronicle of his times the good brother describes a colleague, Brother Giovanni of Ravenna as "fat, corpulent, swarthy—a good, honest man" who was as fond of *lasagne* as he was. Salimbene also remembers the first time he tasted *ravioli*, on the 12th of August, 1284 A.D. "It was on the feast of Saint Clare that I first ate *ravioli* without skin," he wrote.°°

°Antonio Baldini, article in *Il Corriere della Sera*, 9 September 1949: "Pastiera."
°°Salimbene da Parma, *Cronica* a cura di F. Bernini, 12 agosto 1284, 2 vv. Bari, Laterza, 1942.

Antonio Baldini (b. 1889)

The second reference on page 12 provides an interesting reflection on the simple times in which Salimbene lived —when *ravioli*, today an economical dish for the poorest laborer, was looked upon as an extravagant treat. It also

shows that *ravioli* has apparently changed its skin through
the years. Today *ravioli* usually consists of little packets of
dough (skin) filled with minced beef or pork, spinach or
cheese. But *ravioli* may come with or without skin. The
latter is in the older tradition to which Salimbene undoubtedly referred. Artusi, writer of one of the most popular cookbooks in the last hundred years, a work considered a classic of Italian literature, refers to it as "real
ravioli, not made with meat and not wrapped in leaves."°

As Italy emerged from the Middle Ages so emerged
macaroni. In his *Decameron* Boccaccio describes a myth-
ical country of plenty, Bengodi, where no one works and
all the fine things of life are free. The Renaissance Floren-
tine storyteller picked macaroni as a likely symbol of earthly
pleasure.

"In a country called Bengodi," he wrote, "where the
vines are tied up with sausages and a goose is to be had
for a farthing, with a gosling into the bargain, there is a
mountain all made of grated Parmesan cheese On top of
this mountain there are people who do nothing else but
make macaroni and *ravioli*. They cook it in capon broth,
then they toss it down—and those who can grab it may
have all they want and more. Right beside the mountain
is a lovely stream flowing with wine—the best you ever
tasted—and not a drop of water in it."° °

But to Italy macaroni was not only a "divine dish"
and an inspiration to the poet, it also speedily became an
important industry. By 1592 it had become important
enough so that, on December 10th, a Roman law was
passed regulating prices. And, as was the custom in those

°Pellegrino Artusi, *La Scienza in cucina e l'arte di mangiar bene*,
1899, 4th ed. Firenze, Landi, pp. 524.
° °Giovanni Boccaccio, *Decameron*, VIII Day, 3rd story, Bari,
Laterza, 1927 2 vv.

Macaroni-eaters (from the Gatti and Dura Album, Naples)

days, the law-breakers were threatened with the rack, pil-
lory, whip, galley-slavery and other grim tortures.

About this time the macaroni manufacturers formed a
corporation called the *Universitas et Ars Vermicellarum*,
or the University and Art of Vermicelli making. Though
the laws concerning this corporation date from 1642 it
must have existed for many years before. In Rome however,
unlike Bengodi, life was not always simple macaroni and
cheese. The macaroni makers were forever quarreling with
the bakers, originally a part of the corporation, who split
away and squabbled over the competition. They also
quarreled with the vegetable vendors, who also seemed to
feel they were direct competitors; and, curiously, with the
booksellers. For some reason lost to history, the vermicelli
makers of the time were accused of offering books to the
public—illegally.

Naturally no amount of competition could keep macaroni down. In Goldoni's memoirs, the eighteenth-century
playwright depicts a typically lively scene of his time. He
was traveling with friends down the Po River, on a barge,
without a care in the world:

"We laughed, joked, teased each other, and whiled
away the time to no great purpose—until the dinner bell
rang. Then how we ran—macaroni! We fell on it—devoured
it by the three plates full! Then came beef—cold chicken,
loin of veal—and all the wine we could drink, ah! What
a marvelous meal—and what a roaring appetite."°

°Carlo Goldoni, *Memorie di Carlo Goldoni per l'istoria della sua
vita e del suo teatro*, Milano, Sonzogno, 1890, pp. 376.

4

"My Ceccarella's such a dear
See the prize she brings me here
Macaroni steaming nicely
Macaroni sweet and spicy
Macaroni's praise I sing
Here's a dish fit for a king!"
　　　　　　　　—SGRUTTENDIO.*

Of all the areas of Italy it is the region around Naples that is most firmly identified with spaghetti. There are two reasons for this. The first is that throughout the eighteenth century and during the major part of the next hundred years the best products came from Naples and from such little nearby towns as Gragnano and Torre Annunziata. Even today there are those who swear that no macaroni products compare with those from Naples. And the city's great macaroni factories are a major point of interest in this fabulous city.

Naples' place in the history of macaroni-making is

*See page 1.

17

secure. As has been pointed out, the birthplace of spaghetti is a question shrouded in doubt. But there is no
doubt as to where the credit goes for perfecting the process
by which macaroni products were expertly dried to keep
over a long period. As Pasquale Barracano, a director of
the technical magazine *Italian Grain Mills* has said:

"The invention of drying spaghetti is ascertained to
be at the start of the nineteenth century around Naples.
In fact, during this time the first machines were con-
structed for macaroni manufacture. They were made of
wood, based on the theory of a press run by a large
wheel turned by pressure on poles or by a lever pushed
by hand as in the old mills. The spaghetti emerged from
the opening in different sizes—long, short or medium.

"The problem, however, was not one of production,
but that of drying the dough in some reasonable way to
keep it from turning rancid from natural fermentation.
This is done by hanging the dough in the open air, in a
climate where there is frequent change from heat to cold.
Since this change must occur in the shortest space of time,
locations had to be found in which there are maximum
changes of temperature during twenty-four hours. First
Amalfi seemed ideal, then Gragnano. Finally the vicinity
of Torre Annunziata turned out to be the best of all.
There, the climate changes systematically four times a day.
This accounts for the success of macaroni production in
these cities."[*]

Is it any wonder that today some gourmets in New
York will not buy a macaroni unless it comes from Gragnano or from Torre Annunziata? Until the First World
War these were the most highly regarded macaroni names
in this country. Hundreds of thousands of boxes filled

[*]Personal letter from Pasquale Barracano, Rome, February 5, 1952
(Editor of *Molini d'Italia*)

with macaroni in all sizes and shapes were sent to America bearing Gragnano's name.

Describing this product, a nineteenth-century English traveler said:

"The Neapolitan macaroni is easily known by not being twisted like that of Genoa, but straight, or bent only at one end; the reason for this is, that after having been forced out of the press to the usual length, it is cut off, and hung on a stick to dry. The hole of the pipe is very small, and this macaroni never breaks in cooking."[*]

A French observer of the same period, though equally enthusiastic about the quality of the product, added more matter-of-factly: "This point, about the strands not breaking, does an injustice to the manufacturer. What does it matter—when macaroni is not eaten whole anyway?"

Another enthusiast, writing out of a persuasive, if biased, love, sings the enchantment of Neapolitan macaroni in this way:

"The proportions of the semola and farina, the fine qualities in the water, and the good climate give our macaroni the most wonderful odors you ever enjoyed. How many times have the other regions of Italy tried to match this perfection—only to be frustrated by circumstances beyond their control.

"The rich family's custom is to do all kinds of fancy things with the sauce, but the Neapolitan usually eats it savored with white cheese alone. Right beside the big steaming plate of macaroni is a generous portion of cheese in a plate or bowl. From the base to the top of this pyramid-like mound are black strips of pepper. The top is crowned with a tomato or, lacking that vegetable—a red flower."

[*]James Godby, *Italian Scenery, representing the manners, customs and amusements of the different states of Italy,* London, 1823.

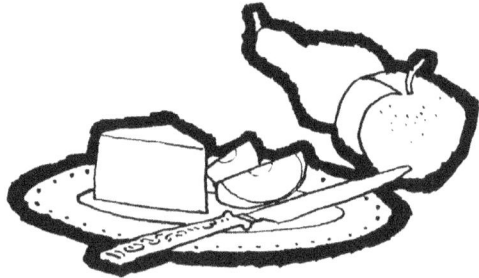

5

*"He fell into it, as the Neapolitan
proverb has it, like macaroni into
the cheese."*

—GIORDANO BRUNO.[*]

Famed as Naples is as a producer of macaroni, it is even
more widely known today as the home of the "macaroni
eater." Reportedly the Neapolitan eats macaroni all the
time. He eats it "at births and at deaths" according to
one writer.[**] According to another:

"Macaroni eaters of all classes are ready to eat macaroni any hour of the day or night—for breakfast, lunch
or dinner. However, I have never succeeded in finding
anyone who eats macaroni on a corpse, as Orazio Vernet
dared to depict in his artistic illustrations of Napoleon's
life. This great passion for such a very simple food can

[*]Giordano Bruno, *Spaccio della Bestia Trionfante*, Opere Italiane,
II, 193? Lanciano, Carabba.
[**]Giuseppe Marotta, article in *Il Corriere della Sera*, 6 November
1948.

People of Naples eating macaroni (from Andrea de Jorio, *La mimica degli antichi investigata nel gestire napoletano,* Napoli, Fibreno, 1832)

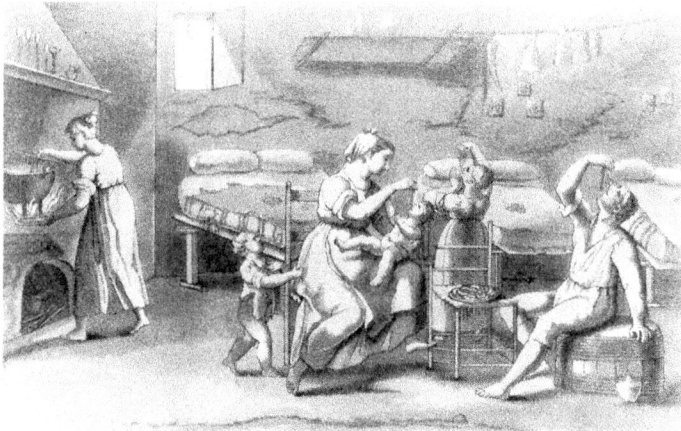

"A me, a me" (from Andrea de Jorio, *La mimica degli antichi investigata nel gestire napoletano,* Napoli, Fibreno, 1832)

be a subject for good-humored joking in Naples, but never anything vituperative or macabre."*

*"Usi e Costumi di Napoli e contorni descritti e dipinti." Opera diretta da Francesco de Bourcard, Napoli, Col. G. Nobile, 1858, vol. 2° pp. 74-5, Capitolo scritto dal Cav. T. Dalbono.

This wholesale and all-absorbing Neapolitan interest in
macaroni as a food did not always prevail. Macaroni eating
did not become widespread in Naples until sometime during the seventeenth century. As Croce was the first to
point out "before this, macaroni had not enjoyed first place
in Neapolitan kitchens. Neapolitans were not called 'macaroni eaters' but 'vegetable eaters.' Macaroni was mentioned
as a Sicilian or Sardinian dish."°

However things were before the seventeenth century,
in that century the legendary "macaroni eater" role was
solidly established as a part of the Neapolitan character.
Canon de Jorio presents an authentic picture of the plebeian
Neapolitan manner of eating macaroni in the seventeenth
century:

"Macaroni can be eaten in separate mouthfuls, as one
eats any other type of food, and as is the custom of eating
at well-bred tables. But the Neapolitan's specialty is the
ability to swallow a whole platterful of macaroni in seem-
ingly one, great uninterrupted gulp. In fact, our celebrated
macaroni-eaters are not those who eat the *most*, but rather,
the greatest quantity at one time—feeding the macaroni
into their mouths with both hands so that there is no
interruption from the time the macaroni enters the mouth
and its arrival in the stomach. This makes macaroni
unique among the various types of food which our poorer
people eat."

The good Canon also tells about the macaroni-eating
contests which took place at the time, similar to the beer-
drinking bouts in Germany:

"Sometimes our fine macaroni-eaters dare to fill themselves with two 'rotoli' (about six pounds) but in the
prescribed way. Two macaroni athletes begin the contest

°Giambattista Basile, Lo Cunto de li cunti, Notes by Benedetto
Croce, Vol. 1, p. 80, note 3. Bari, Laterza, 1939.

Macaroni-eaters (F. Palizzi, 1818-1899)

at the same instant, and provided that neither of them loses his breath, and that both eat the stated amount, the one who gets through the mass first wins the crown..."° Is it any wonder that all an eighteenth-century poet had to do to make his poem sound authentically Italian was to rhyme *lazzaroni*°° with macaroni?

°"Indicazione del più rimarcabile in Napoli e contorni" del canonico D. Andrea de Jorio, Napoli, 1835, pp. 347.
°°beggars

These more extravagant forms of Neapolitan macaroni eating undoubtedly expressed the delight of the poorer worker in finding a food that was cheap to produce, ample in supply and good to eat. But to the original expressions of delight the Neapolitan soon added some theatrical gestures designed to amuse that important creature, the tourist. Every operation of eating macaroni was transformed into a comic spectacle. The hands were raised high in a characteristic pose. The strands slipped down the throat in an almost continuous cascade. The dexterity evidenced years of practice, and the artist went through the whole performance without ever spotting himself.

Thus was born the "macaroni-eater." This soon became the nickname for all Neapolitans and later of all Italians. The authentic "macaroni-eater" is a part of picturesque Naples which every traveler must view before leaving Naples.

One traveler of the nineteenth century took a somewhat dim view of the spectacle.

"The 'mangia macaroni,' or 'macaroni-eater,'" wrote William Stamer of London, "is one of the many objectionable human pests with which the stupidity of a certain class of travelers has inflicted the city. Seeing in the shop windows photographs of impossible *lazzaroni* eating their macaroni 'modo Napolitano,' Brown, Jones and Robinson must needs behold with their own eyes how the feat is accomplished. 'Such fun with the beggars bolting their food like anacondas, and that sort of thing, you know.' So on their return to the hotel, they impart their wishes to their good friend and counsellor, the porter, who hastens to gratify them. The 'mangia macaroni' who seems, like the vulture, to scent his food from afar and to be always at hand when required, is beckoned, a large dish of pasta is given him and, to the delight of the three, he does his best to make a beast of himself by allowing length after

The tavern-keeper (F. Palizzi, 1818-1899)

length to slip down his throat without so much as an attempt at mastication."°

Such theatricalisms of the professional "macaroni-eater" apart, macaroni eating was a central part and an essential pleasure of Neapolitan life. Public houses where nothing but macaroni was sold were called *maccaronare,* and no village was without them. One writer graphically describes the activity that surrounded these places:

"Picture the tavernkeeper as a round, fat fellow, ex-

°William Stamer, *Dolce Napoli*, p. 7, London, 1878.

Maccaronara (Print from the Gatti and Dura Album, Naples, of a Spaghetti House)

pertly distributing the hot macaroni with one hand, deftly sprinkling cheese on top with the other. He is usually surrounded by street urchins, idlers who happen by at the moment, women who want to give a little plate of macaroni to their children, poor people who come to collect alms in the coin of macaroni. Sometimes the macaroni turns red or dark, if the tavernkeeper adds tomato sauce, or a kind of ragout, mixing it with the cheese as he revolves the skein-like vermicelli around and around.

"His fairness in dealing out the macaroni is proverbial, and rarely can anyone accuse him of miscalculation. If he ever slips and adds a few more spaghetti strands to someone's plate, you can be sure his heart had been won over by some adorable child. But no one else intimidates him. Women with their chatter and flattery—tough guys brandishing a stick—querulous characters itching to pick a fight, none of them will ever move him a jot or tittle from the just performance of his duty. He's not a great mathematician, not even an accountant, but numbering macaroni is second nature to him, dividing it is his forte.

"Those who have no time to stay in the *maccaronara* take off their red caps and, depressing the upper part of them, put in the macaroni; which, having paid for, they walk on, and eat as they go; when they have finished they put on the caps again."°

Giuseppe Marotta, Naples' literary interpreter whose works have recently been translated into English, has perhaps said the ultimate word on the close affinity between spaghetti and the Neapolitan:

"He who enters paradise through a door is not a Neapolitan. We make our entrance into that heavenly abode by delicately parting a curtain of spaghetti. As soon as we get weaned from our mother's breast we are fed

°William Stamer, *Dolce Napoli*, London, 1878.

Giuseppe Marotta (b. 1902)

a fragment of spaghetti. . . . What better inheritance can I leave my sons than spaghetti?"°

°Giuseppe Marotta, pamphlet, *Premio Bagutta-Agnesi*, Milano, 12 Gennaio 1949.

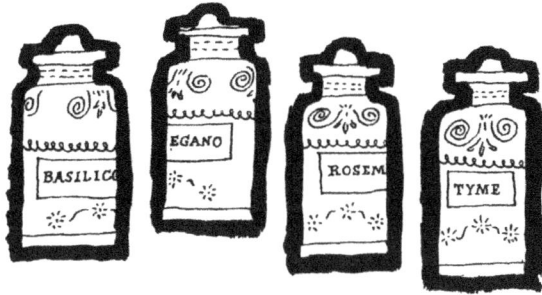

6

"The world's so macaronized grown of late,
That common mortals now are out of date."
—THE MACARONI.*

While in seventeenth-century Naples the figure of the "macaroni-eater" was emerging as that of a ragged, colorful scamp who slipped a whole hatful of spaghetti down his throat in one slither, in London quite another development was taking place. The word "macaroni-eater" was used to designate a really elegant chap who ate imported, costly foods.

The word "macaroni" is found for the first time in English in an Italian-English dictionary put together by John Florio, a Londoner whose father had fled from Italy during the sixteenth century for religious reasons. Florio was no small contributor to international cultural relations, for he translated Montaigne and was well known by Shake-

*The Macaroni, a comedy—as it is performed at the Theatre-Royal in York, MDCCLXXIII, the 2nd ed. Printed by A. Ward.

Title page of second edition
of *The Macaroni: A Comedy*

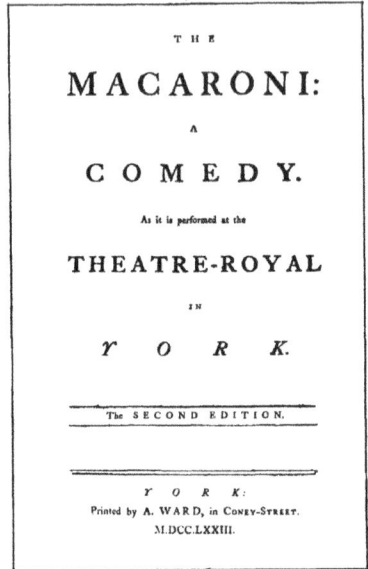

THE

MACARONI:

A

COMEDY.

As it is performed at the

THEATRE-ROYAL

IN

Y O *R* K.

The SECOND EDITION.

Y O *R* K:
Printed by A. WARD, in Coney-Street.
M.DCC.LXXIII.

A
WORLDE
of Wordes,
Or
Moſt copious, and exact
Dictionarie in Italian and
Engliſh, collected by
Iohn Florio.

Printed at London, by
Arnold Hatfield for
Edw. Blount.
1598

Title page of *A Worlde of
Wordes,* 1598

speare. As a matter of fact, all the Italian words which Shakespeare used can be found in Florio's dictionary, which was called *Worlde of Wordes*. There macaroni is defined as a "kind of paste-meate boiled in broth, and drest with butter, cheese and spice."° Paste-meate is his way of saying meal or dough, because he uses it in the same way to describe *vermicelli*. Meat had nothing to do with it.

Vermicélli, *all maner of little wormes or vermin. Alſo a kind of ſmall cut paſte meate they vſe in Italy to make pottage with, & then put grated cheeſe in them.* *as* Tagliarini.

Definition of "vermicelli" from
A Worlde of Wordes

After the Restoration, England was flooded with Italian fashions and customs. Not all the English suddenly went Italian, of course; only the high-born who were accustomed to—and could afford—the niceties of life. They were the *avant-garde* of their day. And they ate macaroni. That is, the well-to-do Londoners did. So did the Royal Family. But not the country folk. The common man regarded macaroni (just as he regarded and probably has always regarded all innovations) with a jaundiced eye. Macaroni was an exotic dish.

There are references to a Macaroni Club in eighteenth-century London. This didn't really exist in the true sense of the word "club." Rather it designated the Café Society of the time.

Says *Scots Magazine* in November, 1772: "Macaroni ... was far from being universally known in this country

° John Florio, *Worlde of Wordes*, published in folio 1598.

The Macaroni by Hogarth

until the commencement of the last peace [1763] when,
like many other foreign fashions, it was imported by our
cognoscenti in eating, as an improvement to the subscrip-

tion table at Almack's [a Café]. In time, the subscribers
to these dinners came to be distinguished by the title of
macaroni and as the meeting was composed of the younger
and gayer part of our nobility and gentry, who, at the
same time that they gave in to our luxuries of eating,
went equally into the extravagancy of dress, the word
macaroni changed its meaning to that of a person who
exceeded the ordinary bounds of fashion, and is now
justly used as a term of reproach of all kinds of people,
indifferently, who fall into the absurdity."

The word, macaroni, also made a transatlantic trip
about this time and, with its meaning of exaggerated
elegance, planted itself in the vocabulary of Colonial America long before the dish which it originally designated
became widely known. Toward the end of the 1700's
Americans were singing about macaroni without knowing,
literally, what it was all about. Their song became famous,
almost a national hymn, and later became established as
the most popular of American folk-songs. The words go:

> "*Yankee Doodle went to town*
> *Riding on a Pony.*
> *He stuck a feather in his cap*
> *And called it* macaroni."

Much research has been done and pet ideas have been
explored to discover the foreign origin of the song—is it
English, German, Dutch? Whatever the origin of the tune,
the words got their inspiration from revolutionary events,
and the song's first appearance, in approximately its established form, can be traced back to 1764. This is just about
the time when *macaroni* in England meant elegant or
dandified. It is not strange that a poet, hunting for a
word to rhyme with *pony* should find *macaroni* ideal for
expressing the elegant touch.

Along this line, we know that two Maryland regiments
with flashy red uniforms (which must really have stood
out beside the average poorly-attired American troops)
were called *macaroni*. They fought valiantly at the Battle
at Breekes Mill by the Gowanus Creek Bridge, Long
Island in 1776. A painting by Alonzo Chappel and a
poem by J. W. Palmer, remain as documents of the impres-
sion they created on the American imagination. The poem
begins:

> *"Spruce Macaronis, and pretty to see,*
> *Tidy and dapper and gallant were we..."**

*Poem by John Williamson Palmer (1825-1906), "The Maryland
Battalion" (Battle of Long Island, Aug. 27, 1776), reproduced from
"Your America Day by Day in Pictures," *New York Journal American*
August 26, 1953.

7

"Here I got the Inspiration for macaroni
And the fairy Mafelina made me a paunchy poet."
—TEOFILO FOLENGO, XVI Century.*

The earliest cookbooks reveal—by omission—that Colonial America was unacquainted with the dish whose name figured so prominently in its most popular song, and which was later to figure so prominently on the national menu. The ignorance was to be corrected shortly but the dish was not to catch on for a long time.

The history of spaghetti in America really begins with that brilliant, enterprising man whose name appears consistently as an innovator in American ideas, activities and institutions. This is so, whether the innovation was in the realm of politics, topography, architecture, mechanics—or the use of foreign foods and condiments. Thomas Jefferson was the first man to import Lombardy poplars, Roman architecture, Tuscan wine (and later the grapevines from that district, from which he made a type of Chianti in his

*Teofilo Folengo (Merlin Cocai), *Le Maccheronee,* a cura di Alessandro Luzio, Bari, Laterza, 1911, 2 vv.

Wood engraving from one of the
first editions of the *Toscolana* by
Folengo showing a woman feeding
gnocchi to her friend, illustrating
the verse: *Imboccare suum veni-
ant macaroni poetam*

garden at Monticello) into America. He was also the first
to import into this country the spaghetti-making machine.

It is possible that Jefferson first became interested in
macaroni when he became Minister to France after the
Revolutionary War and lived in Paris for a time. Italian
cooking had been well known in Paris since the days of
the Renaissance when it made its debut there along with
the paintings of Leonardo da Vinci and Parmigianino.

On the other hand he could have already sampled this
Italian food in a restaurant in Richmond near his home.
His expense accounts show that he had a charge account
with one Serafino Formica, or Formicola, an innkeeper of
Venetian and Neapolitan origin, who ran a Richmond inn.
Serafino had come to America as the *maître d'hotel* of
Lord Dunmore, and claimed to be a descendant of a
Venetian doge. Whatever the merits of that claim, he was

Macaroni-eaters, 1885. Attributed to Mataria

certainly a Neapolitan (or part-Neapolitan) and would certainly have prepared spaghetti. And the records do show that Jefferson did eat in his establishment both before and after his trip to France.

In 1787 Jefferson left Paris for the express purpose of making a trip to Italy to do a bit of exploring—and smuggling. He had a distinctly patriotic motive—he wanted to bring back an Italian machine which he had heard could husk rice without breaking the kernels. A gourmet, he knew

Thomas Jefferson

how rice should be served—light and fluffy, with the intact kernels delicately separated one from the other—not all congealed together in an unappetizing mess. In addition to the machine he also wanted to bring back Piedmontese rice, a superior rice which stood up sturdily in the process of cooking.

In Jefferson's day the export of this finer type of rice was forbidden. Manufacturing and agricultural methods were secrets as closely guarded by governments as our atomic secrets are today, and severe penalties—even death— were imposed on rice smugglers. This didn't stop Jefferson from bribing a muleteer into giving him the precious rice, and he crossed the Alps back into France without incident—and with a couple of bags of rice in his pocket.

Before leaving Italy in this rather unorthodox way, Jefferson made a fifteen-day expedition through Piedmont, Lombardy and Liguria. Now he was in search of the reported macaroni-making machine. He made careful notes in his diary about the people, the culture and the vineyards he came across. His observations during his Italian visit show what a really inquiring spirit he had—fresh, keen, continually spurred on by his curiosity. His attention was drawn both to ancient monuments and to modern inventions and he regarded everything with an almost reverent interest. His most serious attention was devoted to the cultivation of such products as almonds, capers and olives. And always he kept up his pursuit of the macaroni machine.

Though unsuccessful on this trip he continued his search by proxy. He wrote to his friend and secretary, William Short, then touring Italy. He advised him to visit Virgil's tomb but not to be carried away by the typical guide's tale that the laurel bush nearby had flourished in the poet's time. He also urgently requested him to keep on the look-out for the macaroni machine, and to find out how it worked.

In due time Short was able to reply:

"I procured at Naples according to your request, the mould for making macaroni. ... it is of smaller diameter than is used in the manufactories of macaroni, but of the diameter that had been sent to gentlemen in other countries. I went to see the macaroni made. The machine for pressing (*trafila*) as used at Naples is enormous—much more so than I had expected. The price they told me for fitting up one of these machines with the mortar, etc. was the value of 100 *louis d'or*. The depth of the mortar is about 20 or 24 inches. . . . The width of the mortar that you desired to know is marked on the mould you will receive . . . it was left with my banker at Naples to be forwarded to you. . . ."°

Thus the macaroni machine came to America.

Despite Jefferson's intervention, however, spaghetti eating was not to take hold in this country for a long, long time. Spaghetti is mentioned in a 1792 cookbook, but the advice given is to cook it in water for three hours, then recook it in broth for ten minutes. Finally, says the recipe, it should be mixed with bread in a soup tureen!

If Americans believed that this was the way to serve spaghetti, it is no wonder that spaghetti was rarely served!

Apart from the distaste which such a culinary horror must have produced, spaghetti had to overcome the almost universal tendency to look upon foreign foods as highly suspect, akin to foreign spies. Before spaghetti could become really American it had to have a lot of publicity, the endorsement of famous people, the absorption of the Italian population with older-stock Americans, and the ascent of the Italians on the social and financial scale of American life. In short, spaghetti had to be assimilated. . . slowly.

°Letter to Jefferson from William Short, 11 February 1789 in *Jefferson's Writings*.

8

"Oh where is the might
The famous, thrilling sight
of parading macaroni?
Who—sparkling, clean and light
Marched by with joy and mirth
And appeared to own the earth?"
—CARNIVAL SONG.[*]

Spaghetti did not really begin to establish its position as part of the American cuisine—and then but slowly—until after the middle of the nineteenth century. Then Americans in ever increasing numbers began to travel to Europe and to Italy. There many of them tasted, for the first time, spaghetti as it should be cooked, and learned how to roll the strange new food around their forks. Certainly when they came back they brought not only a new appreciation for the Italian arts and the Italian's easy way of life, but they also brought back recipes for cooking, seasoning and serving the foreign food. And these began to spread around.

It took, however, a major cultural upheaval in Ameri-

[*]Pietro Martorana, *Canti Carnevaleschi napoletani,* 1850, p. 58.

41

Macaroni-eater (from the Gatti and Dura Album, Naples)

can life before spaghetti became the mass consumption item it is today. The event which brought this about produced many changes in the American mode of life. It was prohibition. With prohibition came the speakeasy. In more or less dimly lit basement speakeasies, Americans could find wine, more or less palatable, made by an Italian, more or less legally. And what would the Italian serve to go with his wine? What else but his national dish? Thus, proper spaghetti was informally introduced to millions of Americans. And the march was on.

That macaroni and spaghetti had really become part of American culture was signalized by their long-deferred entrance into American literature and art. In one of Damon Runyon's stories there appears the character, "The Macarone":

" 'Why,' Chesty Charles says 'do my eyes deceive me, or do I behold The Macarone out of Kansas City?' The Macarone seems to be an interesting character in many respects and I can see that he and Charles know each other from several places. . . ."*

Naturally, The Macarone is probably a dark and swarthy Italian. He may even be tall for a change. But, considering that this is a Damon Runyon story, it should be pointed out that The Macarone turns out to be not such a bad fellow. As luck would have it, he does not murder after all. He finds the man he's supposed to kill—a suicide—and everything ends reasonably happily.

America's artistic celebration of spaghetti is not, however, primarily a literary one. It was the movies—quite a natural medium for a new element in American life—which

*Damon Runyon, "A Job for the Macarone" in *The Damon Runyon Omnibus,* Garden City, Sun Dial Press, 1944, pp. 505.

first recognized this developing American institution. The artist principally responsible is Charlie Chaplin.

Spaghetti shines in all its glory of sauce, butter and cheese in innumerable of Chaplin's films, most notably in two classic scenes. In *City Lights* a tipsy millionaire gets tangled up in the spaghetti strands, smears his face and ends up fighting the mess. And in the most poignant scene in *The Gold Rush*, Chaplin, in love and starving, pretends that his sweetheart's shoe-strings are spaghetti and starts to eat them. In this way, the Italian dish is given both comic and pathetic roles in American films. More importantly, it is used as an element of the American scene which will instantly be recognized by millions of American movie goers.

Italian artists—principally of the theatre—played a prominent part in spreading the popularity of spaghetti through the early decades of this century. The renown of spaghetti in this period was, for example, definitely tied to the fame of New York's Metropolitan Opera.

America is a democratic country, where the power of the masses is enormous. But it is also a country where the individual personality counts a great deal. A person who makes a name for himself in one field can reflect his glory and extend his influence through many unrelated fields. Several of the famous tenors and prima donnas who have been favorites with the American public have been Italians and their love of spaghetti was widely advertised. But the one of these who did more than all the others to make spaghetti a household staple was Enrico Caruso.

At the height of his career Caruso was adored almost as a god and as a benefactor of humanity. His every act, on this or the far side of the famous Golden Curtain, was always a subject of widespread comment and appraisal. Even now his voice lives on through his records—not accurately, unfortunately, because in those early days it was impossible to catch all the refinements and nuances of tone. And his name continues to be listed among the immortals of song.

Caruso was from Naples and, naturally, he loved his spaghetti dearly. Like many Italian men he was proud of his reputation as a cook, and vain enough to show off his talents whenever the opportunity presented itself. His passion for fine cooking was well known and his appetite legendary. Encouraged by universal adulation he would agree to show restaurateurs, from time to time, his way of cooking and seasoning spaghetti.

One of the times he did this was fully reported in the newspapers. It happened at the Hotel York where Caruso went into the kitchen to supervise personally the preparation of spaghetti for some friends. Caruso made a sauce with tomatoes, basil, parsley, red pepper, and olive oil in which garlic had been fried. He gold-dusted the macaroni with Parmesan cheese, and decorated it with coins of fried zucchini squash. Through this and similar dishes Caruso and spaghetti became identified in the public mind and his fame added to its renown. Apparently there is no end to the publicity his name will give it.

The pianist, Artur Rubinstein, gives this colorful account of Caruso: "In New York we had dinner together almost every night. When we entered the Italian restaurant, everyone recognized him [Caruso] and would stop to see how he was going to manage with the spaghetti. One evening he became infuriated, threw down his fork, took a fistful of macaroni *alla pommarola* [Neapolitan for tomato sauce] with his hands, held it up high over his face, then let it drop into his open mouth, staining his face, tie, vest and jacket with the sauce. I loved that man Caruso! He had a heart of pure gold—just like his voice."[*]

[*]Incontri—Rubinstein, *Corriere della Sera*, 5 December 1954, p. 3. Article by Indro Montanelli.

A caricature of Gioacchino Rossini with a large spaghetti bib,
in Radiciotti's life of Rossini

Other singers have cemented the alliance between spaghetti and Italian music. Reportedly they consider it useful in developing their stomach and chest muscles. Rosa Ponselle, the former Metropolitan diva, has created her own recipe, which she calls "Spaghetti a la mama," or "spaghetti just like mother used to make." Among currently popular singers, Mario Lanza is said to feel that he must eat spaghetti in order to sing well.

Of course, in Italy, too, stories abound about the affinity between spaghetti and singers, musicians and writers. The celebrated restaurateur Canaveri is said to have commented after a culinary argument with Gioacchino Rossini: "Don't know the name. But if that man knows his music like he knows his macaroni, he must be a damn good composer!"* Of Rossini it is also told that once he was asked by a neighbor at a dinner party if he remembered

*Giuseppe Radiciotti, *Gioacchino Rossini, Vita documentata, Opere ed influenza su l'arte*, Vol. II, p. 356. Tivoli, Arti Grafiche Majella di Aldo Chicca, 1927, 3 vv.

him. "I sat next to you at a dinner in your honor when they served a huge macaroni pie" the man said. "I remember the macaroni," Rossini replied, "but I don't seem to remember you."*

Maybe these stories are apocryphal, but there is nothing apocryphal about the role Italian-American musicians are known to have played in bringing to the attention of the American people the delights of the spaghetti dinner.

*Giuseppe Radiciotti, *Aneddoti rossiniani*, Roma, Formiggini, 1929.

9

"The macaroni industry has become permanently established (in America) in the last forty years. It was a minor industry prior to World War I, when citizens were just beginning to realize macaroni products were a desirable and wholesome food."

—HENRY C. PUTNAM.[*]

In New York, just after the First World War, another artist—this one a sculptor named Attilio Piccirilli—used to prepare spaghetti in his studio with the aid of a then little-known figure from the tough, explosive world of New York politics. That figure was Fiorello La Guardia. Apart from his other claims to fame he was to play an important but uncelebrated role in helping the spaghetti industry become a full, legal and responsible citizen of the United States.

[*]Executive Secretary, Northwest Crop Improvement Association. Minneapolis, Minn.

48

Art and politics met in Fiorello La Guardia. He was possessed of a genius for the dramatic, a sharp, irascible spirit, and a fighting drive to establish the things he believed in. With his short, squat figure, his over-size hat, his strident voice so often vituperating and criticizing, and his profound honesty, he speedily became a commanding political personality and a powerful political force.

La Guardia's name is linked with the American history of spaghetti in a political rather than an artistic way, though he, too, left a spaghetti recipe to posterity. When he was a Congressman (a very curious kind of American Congressman, by the way, now in one party, now in the other, and once outside both major parties for a time) he began to look into the situation in the then rapidly developing spaghetti industry, concerning himself with the health of the public and the honesty of the spaghetti business.

During and immediately after World War I, the American spaghetti producing industry had sprung into being. Before the great conflagration, the United States had imported from Italy up to 76,881,086 pounds of macaroni a year. By 1919 this figure had been reduced to 29,717,000 and the United States began actually to *export* the food.

After the war, this new American industry wished to protect itself against a possible resurgence of Italian competition. It asked for and obtained a tariff. The industry was, at that time, mainly in Italian-American hands but commerce is no respecter of nationalities. As people of other national origins joined in the manufacture of macaroni, the industry became more definitely American. One Italian-American manufacturer[*] who was working in the industry at the time recalls that before the First World

[*]Thomas A. Cuneo, President of Nat. Food Dist. Ass. 1950, in *Macaroni Journal*.

Special label for macaroni exported to the U. S., 1906

War all the correspondence dealing with the macaroni industry was carried on in Italian; ten years later it had changed over completely to English.

The Americanization of the industry was accompanied by a distinct industrial change. In the early days spaghetti-making took place for the most part in one big, poorly-lighted room containing the three machines necessary to macaroni manufacture. The machines in those days were usually manned by members of one family who sold their product principally to other Italian-American families, generally from the same little section of Italy as the spaghetti-makers.

When the thriving industry began producing for the growing mass market, it entered the machine age of mass

Machinery and workers for macaroni products in the eighteenth century (from Paul-Jacques Malouin, *Descriptions et détails des arts du meunier, du vermicellier et du boulanger*, Paris, Saillant et Nyon, 1767, through the courtesy of the Bibliothèque Nationale of Paris)

production. The American industrial system moved in to
put spaghetti on the assembly line. There were machines
to roll out the dough, knead it, press and cut it, pack the
spaghetti in cardboard boxes, and later wrap these in
cellophane. These boxes were shipped to distant stores by
truck and train. Modern inventions made the factory a
cleaner, healthier place to work in. They also made it
possible to guarantee a uniform, high quality of product.

Unfortunately, during the depression, the prices of
macaroni products fell to such a low level that it was
difficult to make them economically with the necessary
grains, or with the prescribed hygienic precautions. As a
result *Egg Fettuccine,* for example, was likely not to contain
any eggs, and artificial coloring took their place. *Ravioli*
contained less meat. Moreover the smaller firms did not
hesitate to cheat on weight, cutting the contents of one-
pound boxes to twelve ounces, then to ten, and finally to
eight.

La Guardia was one of the collaborators on the enactment of the Federal F.D.C. Act which required manufacturers to supply not only their names and addresses, but
also the net weight and ingredients of the contents, on
their packages. The law also attempted to set up standards
for merchandise which until then had been sold without
any guarantee or responsibility. Every type of macaroni
was clearly defined in precise legal terms.

"Macaroni Products," said the act, "are the class of
food each of which is prepared by drying formed units
of dough made from semolina, flour, farina, or any
combination of two or more of these, with water and with
or without one or more of the optional ingredients specified
in sub-paragraphs (1) to (5) inclusive. . . .

"Macaroni is the macaroni product the units of which
are tube-shaped and more than 0.11 inch but not more than
0.27 inch in diameter . . .

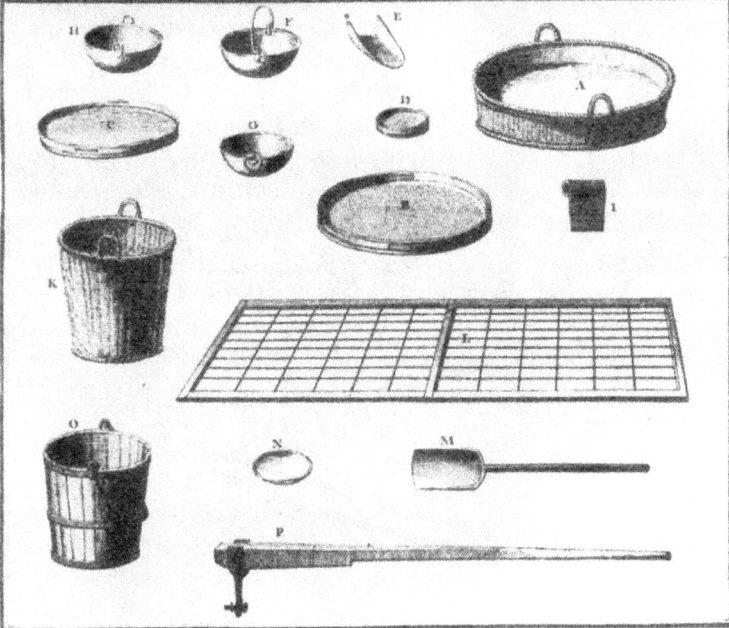

Instruments for making dough, and women working in a shop of the
eighteenth century (from Paul-Jacques Malouin, *Descriptions et
détails des arts du meunier, du vermicellier et du boulanger*, Paris,
Saillant et Nyon, 1767, through the courtesy of the Bibliothèque
Nationale of Paris)

"Spaghetti is the macaroni product the units of which are tube-shaped or cord-shaped (not tubular) and more than 0.06 inch but not more than 0.09 inch in diameter."[*]

These are examples. They reflect the attempt made to protect the consumer from misleading advertising, and to protect the manufacturer from dishonest competition. The legislation has been useful in stopping frauds of both kinds. The possibility exists that through too rigid standardization it might end in frustrating progress in the way of new improvements, fresh research into new and improved macaroni products. American inventive genius has met, and undoubtedly will continue to meet and overcome, that hazard.

Apart from its social effects, the law had an important historical significance. Its enactment meant that the spaghetti industry had become American—standardized in a positive sense, cleaner, healthier, responsible for creating ready-to-eat cooked products for the American and world markets. Spaghetti was an Italian creation. America converted it into something new and big and growing, as American as the skyscraper.

[*]Federal Security Agency, Federal Food, Drug and Cosmetic Act. Part. 16, no. 21, Issued Aug. 1939. Revised, March 1949.

10

"One of the dishes served at the Duchess of Windsor's ball, held earlier this winter (1952) at the Waldorf-Astoria Hotel for the benefit of the hospitalized veteran's music service, was a so-called crown of spaghetti with mushrooms. It was created with a bow to one of the four sponsors of the party, the Buitoni Foods Corporation, manufacturers of pasta. The dish exemplified an un-Italian way of presenting a pasta. But for the very reason that the recipe is more American than Italian, many home cooks are sure to seize on it...."

—JANE NICKERSON.[*]

In addition to its role in streamlining the production of macaroni products, America has made a most important contribution to spaghetti history through research. It is still opening up new ways of producing, seasoning and presenting spaghetti to the world. A major contribution in this field has been the growth of hard grains in the

[*]*New York Times,* January 1953.

55

vast fields of the American West. Hard grains—always
considered the best—are now legally required for spaghetti
production in the United States.

Durum—or hard grain—is not natively an American
grain. The word is a Latin one, but the grain was fairly
well-known in the times of the ancient Greeks who
described it as hard, transparent and yellowish. (Today,
official grain standards of the United States say that the
best durum wheat should be amber-colored.) Even in
those days its high nutritional value was recognized, for
Galen, the founder of the medical profession who lived
in the second century, found the grain so compact and
hard he was sure, as soon as he bit into it, that it would
make a more nutritious bread than other grains. Although
Galen was court physician to the Roman Emperor, Marcus
Aurelius, it was another Roman Emperor, Vespasian, who
is credited with first having imported durum wheat into
Rome.

According to the story, Vespasian imported it from
Russia, for Russia, at that time, as until very recently, was
the principal source of durum wheat. Several attempts
were made to grow the wheat successfully in the United
States but none were satisfactory until, in 1943, Professor
M. A. Carleton of the Department of Agriculture took a
hand in the problem.

Professor Carleton wanted to find a strong, disease-
resistant grain to take the place of American grain which
had fallen victim to black rot. He began to import the
Kubanka type of durum wheat from Russia. Carleton
was the apostle of hard grains. He went to the farmer to
convince him that the new grain would save him from
ruin; he persuaded the miller that the new grain really
had a future; he promoted the new hard grain among hotel
chefs. He had the product analyzed and appraised by
chemists to demonstrate its high nutritive value. He took

Professor M. A. Carleton, 1936 (through the courtesy of H. A. Rodenhiser of the U. S. Dep't of Agriculture)

every necessary step to make this grain a success. And he won.

Thanks to Dr. Carleton's energy and stick-to-it-iveness America became a principal producer of the hard durum wheat grain. The Dakotas were changed from pastoral and breeding lands into one of the richest grain basins in the country. Today around thirty-five million bushels of durum are harvested each year, and hard grain has become an important export. Even Italy today receives grain from America for her macaroni products.

11

"Music is like spaghetti. If you like spaghetti you do not eat it morning, noon and night. You only have it once in a while. It should be kept distant so that you have a real hunger for it."
—DIMITRI MITROPOULOS.

So America finally had spaghetti. It could produce the best wheat grains. It had perfected the process of manufacturing macaroni products. It had a population convinced of the nutritional values of macaroni, willing to eat it and eager to enjoy it. It had those signs all over the land inviting the people to a "spaghetti dinner."

But along with spaghetti, which it had imported from Italy, America acquired a problem, which still troubles many people. How do you eat it?

The answer is that it can be eaten in many different ways, according to the disposition of the one who is dining. The spaghetti may be neatly arranged with a fork. It may be assisted onto the fork with a spoon and then bounced into the mouth at one clip. Or it may be strung into the mouth like an unruly skein of wool.

An Italian can tell from the way you eat spaghetti whether you are a foreigner, or a foreigner who has learned the spaghetti-eating art. An astute Italian can even tell traits of character—whether one is greedy, miserly, quick-thinking, shy, impetuous, cautious, disorderly, or just distracted by the way you get to work on the spaghetti which the waiter or your host has set before you.

Actually, there are many ways to solve the problem of eating a plate of spaghetti. You can attack it boldly, or play around with the strands at the end of your fork. You can decide to approach it from right field—or left. Dive straight in from the top, if you wish. Or—do nothing for a while and let the spaghetti cool off, thereby committing the worst sin in the spaghetti gourmet's book.

To use or not use a fork? Right hand or left? What about the spoon? Should you twirl the fork? Should you use a knife to cut the strings that hang down—or would a spoon be better?

All of this is nonsense. The purpose of eating is enjoyment—not conformity with conventions. Because of their English heritage Americans put too much stock in good manners or, rather, accepted eating conventions. The true macaroni eater is never embarrassed when a slip occurs, whether he makes it or you do. He laughs. Even if a drop of tomato sauce falls on the tablecloth or on a guest's shirt, the macaroni lover laughs about it. This dish is frankly popular and easy-going, probably the most cordial and convivial dish in the world.

12

"Dica, signor, come li vuole, al dente?"

There remains, before we turn to our anthology of spaghetti
dinner recipes, the burning question of *al dente*, which
agitates all lovers of spaghetti. How do you know when the
spaghetti is done? How firm should it be? How, in short,
can you insure a perfectly cooked spaghetti?

"When we were very young," write the authors of
one cookbook, "we knew some Italian families who had a
fascinating method of testing their spaghetti. The mother
would take a few lengths of the spaghetti on a fork and
hurl it at the wall over the sink. If the spaghetti stuck to
the wall it was done."**

Thomas Jefferson, in his book of household recipes,
had a partial answer to the question of *al dente*. He

*Beginning of a sonnet in Italo-American jargon "Say, sir, how you
want them; firm?" *Prodotto Italiano,* May 1952.
**You Can Cook if You Can Read* by Muriel and Cortland
Fitzsimmons. New York, Viking Press, 1946.

advised fifteen minutes in boiling salted water for
tagliatelle. He left the cooking time for spaghetti, however,
to the individual's judgment. "Until tender," he said.

Gradually the cooking time accepted by American
cooks has been shortened and the resulting improvement
in taste has been noticeable. Mary Martewen, cooking
editor of the *Chicago Evening American,* wrote in 1933
that tenderness was not to be confused with flabbiness.
"Spaghetti that has been cooked too long becomes soft and
shapeless, losing its taste appeal."° In recent years some
Americans, feeling that they had by now become macaroni
connoisseurs, have taken to invoking that untranslatable
phrase, *al dente.* "Just bitable" or "Just cutable with a fork"
are only approximations of the meaning. To be *al dente,*
the macaroni can't be soft or mushy. Neither can it be
underdone or hard. When the macaroni is cooked *just*
to the point where it can be bitten—not too hard, not too
soft—it's *al dente,* literally "to the tooth," actually "just
right." Which leaves the poor cook exactly where she was.

It is well to remember that the Neapolitans—with
whom the phrase is most closely associated—like their
spaghetti somewhat on the hard side. Perhaps this predi-
lection is due to the advice of a famous Neapolitan gourmet,
the Duke of Bonvicino, whose advice for cooking macaroni,
while general, is still good: use water that is boiling
furiously, and remove the macaroni from the water just at
the moment when there is still a bit of resistance to the
fork when you try to cut through a strand. Or, in the words
of Cristoforo de Messisburgo of the 16th century, cook it
"long enough to say a short prayer."°°

It must be recognized that there is plenty of kitchen

°*Chicago Evening American,* 1933.
°°Cristoforo de Messisburgo, *Banchetti,* 1549.

work involved before a good spaghetti dinner can be produced. This is the real obstacle which troubles most Americans—the bother of making their spaghetti dinner good. To involve them in this project would mean their acceptance of a very important point—that good macaroni is well worth the time spent in the kitchen. The difficulty of persuading them of this is clear when you consider that almost all cookbooks on the market place their major emphasis on speed and simplicity.

Today, it is true, preparing a spaghetti dinner can be quick and easy. There are plenty of spaghettis in tins or glass jars, swimming in sauce, and even accompanied with meat balls. Some of these remain on the shelves for months, even years. It is one of the wonders of modern science that they are still tasty after long periods of confinement. It is also possible to procure frozen *lasagne* which are as good as most cooks can make. Good as these can be, and convenient for the unexpected guest, they fail to involve that artistic stimulation which stirs the cook when faced with raw macaroni.

There is a half-way measure. The American housewife can get her creative thrill by buying one of the packages which contain all the elements of a macaroni or a spaghetti dinner separately. All she has to do is to pour out the contents, and cook.

Acknowledgments

"They say late thanks are ever best" declaimed Bacon; and it is at the end of this work that the author wishes to acknowledge the help he received. Although this volume is not primarily scholarly, it required research, reading and photostating, both here and in Europe. So the author thanks his friends and correspondents, institutions of learning, libraries and museums. They are, if memory serves well: The United States Department of Agriculture (Mr. H. A. Rodenhiser, Beltsville, Maryland); the West Point Museum; the Bibliothèque Nationale, Paris; Prof. Edmondo Cione, University of Naples; Miss Anita Mondolfo, Chief Librarian of the Biblioteca Nazionale Centrale, Florence; the National Macaroni Institute (Mr. Robert Green, Palatine, Illinois); Prof. Paolo Toschi, University of Rome; Museum of Science and Industry, Chicago; Massachusetts Institute of Technology, Cambridge; the Library of Princeton University; Thomas Jefferson Memorial Foundation, Charlottesville; Maryland Historical Society, Baltimore; Domenico Petrocelli, writer, Naples; Ing. Vincenzo Agnesi, macaroni manufacturer, Oneglia; Mr. Pasquale Barracano, editor of *Molini d'Italia*, Rome; Braibanti and Co., macaroni machine makers, Milan; Daisy Fornacca, Florence;

63

64   Spaghetti Dinner

Food Research Institute, Stanford University; Dr. B. Fava, Librarian of the Biblioteca Comunale, Reggio dell'Emilia; South Dakota State College, Brookings; Mr. Anthony Gisolfi, teacher, New York; Virginia Historical Society, Richmond.

Also Northwestern Crop Improvement Association, Minneapolis; Dr. Ferdinand Maurino, Dickinson College, Carlisle, Penna.; Biblioteca Nazionale Vittorio Emanuele II, Rome; North Dakota Agricultural College, Fargo; Mario Monti, writer and editor, Milan; Dr. Miraglia, Florence; and many others the author may have bothered and not here mentioned. The authors, publishing houses and food editors that were kind enough to help in compiling this Anthology of Recipes have been mentioned in the appropriate places and here are all thanked again in unison.

The author wishes that he could also give a list of semantic works, especially those published in Italy, which have enlarged and enlightened the history of macaroni products. Names such as Messedaglia, Schiaffini, Paoli, Goidanich would lead all the rest.

I should mention the help received from members of the Buitoni family and from their staff in New York. A full list would be too long; an exception, however, must be made in the case of Miss Joan E. Thimm, chemist consultant of Buitoni, Hackensack. In technical matters her advice was invaluable.

Various ways, old and new, of making, cooking, and seasoning spaghetti, for fun, curiosity and use. Foreign as well as American recipes, regional and national, favorites of famous presidents, of popes, and of the common man. Taken from ancient books and from modern ones, from newspapers and magazines, borrowed, invented, discovered, adapted, always with the hope of tickling the taste and stimulating the spirit of adventure in some reader.

How to Cook Spaghetti

Cooking spaghetti and other products of the same family, called by Italians *paste alimentari*, is, in many ways, the simplest thing in the world. Always use a great deal of slightly salted boiling water. Bring the water to a fast boil. Add spaghetti gradually. Stir occasionally to prevent the spaghetti from sticking to the sides or bottom of the saucepan. Do not use a lid. Drain the spaghetti and serve with sauce. Let your guests add cheese to taste. You never can tell; there are people who actually dislike cheese. It is unfortunate but possible; and you must be prepared for just such an emergency.

It is difficult to supply a satisfactory answer to the question of how long to cook spaghetti. The answer depends on the thickness and quality of the product, *and* on the taste of the eater. If later it is to go into the oven to be baked, it is best not to boil it too long. It seems almost elementary to say that thin spaghetti needs less cooking time than thick macaroni; the perforated kind cooks more rapidly than the plain string type; old spaghetti, being tougher, takes longer to cook than fresh.

The best way to tell if spaghetti is done to your own personal taste, or to your family's liking, is to sample

a piece of it. Many housewives in Italy are adept at pressing the spaghetti with a spoon or fork against the side
of the saucepan and judging if it is done by the degree
of pressure resistance.

Old Italo-American families like the kind of spaghetti
that takes a long time to cook. The resistance of the
dough to the boiling water is considered a proof of its
quality: the harder the better. In general, Italians like
spaghetti to be solid between their teeth, or chewy, *al
dente* they call it. If it is too soft it tastes like squash
to them, and they don't like squash. Many Americans who
have been to Italy now accept the *al dente* way, but
generally Americans prefer their spaghetti a bit softer. In
the recipes that follow, the original instruction for the
length of time for boiling spaghetti has been allowed to
stand. The responsibility is the author's and yours.

Spaghetti, macaroni, elbows, etc., and almost all of
even the fancier forms of *paste*, are alike in that the same
general cooking principles can be applied to all of them.
What applies to spaghetti applies also to elbows. Cook
until you like the texture. The only exceptions are the
very small forms of *paste* which are ordinarily cooked
alone in broth, or with fresh vegetables; or the large types
like *rigatoni, lasagne*, which can be filled with almost
anything; meat, ham, fish, ricotta or other cheese, or even
nuts.

The exigencies of modern living have called forth
fast-cooking brands of spaghetti. So, you can get on the
market certain kinds of *spaghettini* (thin spaghetti) which
can be cooked in three minutes. These apart, the cooking
time generally for spaghetti is from seven to fifteen minutes, depending on taste. It is not advisable to keep even
medium-thick spaghetti in boiling water more than fifteen
minutes.

In some of the recipes that follow you will be told

that an eight-ounce package makes three or four servings. It may; but don't count on it. You must consider the imagination and capacity of your guests. A person of large girth or heavy appetite may find eight ounces just right for himself alone, and even want more after almost licking the plate.

The variety of forms combined with the variety of sauces makes a versatile food out of spaghetti. There is even an incentive to invent new combinations and to create new presentations. Try your own recipe and name it after yourself. You may even win a prize from the Macaroni Association. Spaghetti mixes well with meat, fish, clams, poultry, cheese, fruit and vegetables, and may be served for any course: as an appetizer with anchovy sauce, as a salad with green broccoli, as an *entree* with meat balls, as a dessert with sugar and cinnamon.

The sauces that can be used vary greatly, as you will see in this anthology. But the classic one is still that made with tomato paste cooked in olive oil with onion and garlic. And the classic cheese to sprinkle over it is the Parmesan. However, Southern Italians prefer the pungent Pecorino, and many Americans even use Cheddar. Nothing is alien to spaghetti. It can really be called the good mixer of the table.

Some Ingredients for a Basic Sauce

TOMATO   Fresh or in cans. The best peeled tomatoes are imported from Italy. Tomato paste is the most widely used base. This is to be dissolved in water and put to simmer for an hour or so, with browned onions and garlic to taste.

BASIL   (Italian *basilico*) This odorous herb is to be found fresh only in Italian markets in late spring or early summer. It can be cultivated easily in gardens or in pots. Dried basil can be found in jars everywhere but it hasn't the character of the fresh.

OREGANO   This is a very odorous plant, the petals of which are very easily preserved and available in dried form.

WINE   All dry white wines, if high in alcoholic content, like Sherry, may be added to the sauce. Sometimes red wines, like Burgundy, mix well. Never use sweet wines, like Muscatel or Sauterne. Add the dry wine at the last minute, not more than two minutes before turning off the heat. Proportions vary according to taste; two teaspoonsful per person is a reasonable standard. Contrary to the opinion of teetotalers, the wine leaves no trace of alcohol; only a bouquet.

GLUTA-MATE OF SODIUM   Sold under various names, this improves the taste of all sauces.

ONION AND GARLIC   These are the oldest, most respectable, and most popular condiments of any spaghetti sauce. If you like them, dice them and leave them in the sauce; if you like them a little less but recognize their importance, cut them in large pieces (for

the garlic use a clove) and, after they are
brown, remove them from the butter or oil.
Then add the tomato or diluted tomato paste.

The onion must be cooked very slowly, or as
the Italians say, on the flame of a match; it
becomes almost dissolved in the olive oil or
butter; and must never become black or burn;
the color the painter-cook should strive for is
amber.

Maccaronaro

An International Anthology of Recipes for a Spaghetti Dinner

Original Italian Recipes

The oldest recipes for spaghetti are Italian, and they date from the time of Dante. Some such recipes are included here not for any practical purpose but as examples of customs. They give directions on how to make a good dough rather than the way to cook it. In more recent years the traditional seasoning has been butter and cheese; but occasionally the dough was mixed with spice and honey, and the food used as a dessert. One of the recipes proves that many years ago the small-size spaghetti was cut in various original shapes and even in the form of an alphabet, just as it is today.

Tortelli

You can mold paste in any shape—horse shoes, buckles, rings, letters of the alphabet and any animal you like. And if you wish, you can fill it and cook it in a saucepan with lard, oil and fish, and color it as you like.

> —From *Il libro della cucina*, XIV century, by F. Zambrini, 1863.

Lasagne

If you wish to make lasagne for Lent, cook them. Take clean shelled well-crushed and chopped nuts and fill them in the lasagne. When cooking, keep the smoke away from them. Before serving, dust them with spice and sugar.

—From *Il libro di cucina del sec. XIV*,
Leghorn, Giusti 1899.

Quinquinelli (or very good ravioli)

If you want to make these, shell and crush almonds and add sugar. If you are preparing them for a time when meat can be eaten, mix meat with the almonds and prepare them as you would ravioli and fry them in good shortening. When they are fried, keep them warm.

—From *Il libro di cucina del sec. XIV*,
Leghorn, Giusti 1899.

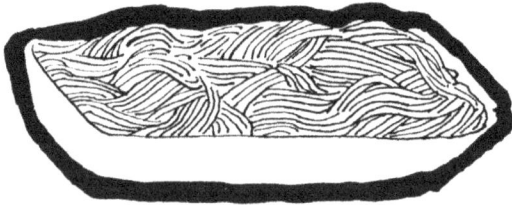

Macaroni

Macaroni is served as a first dish. I beseech you though to cook it firmly (very firmly so that it is as crisp as fresh green salad) and put it in the pot when the water is really boiling (I must tell you how a cook vexed his employer by serving him macaroni that had been put in the pot before the water boiled. The macaroni, which became all sticky, was totally deprived of any flavor. To see if this is really so, try it some morning and may the truth win).

—From Ippolito Cavalcanti, Duca di Buonvicino's *Cook Book*, Naples, 1839.

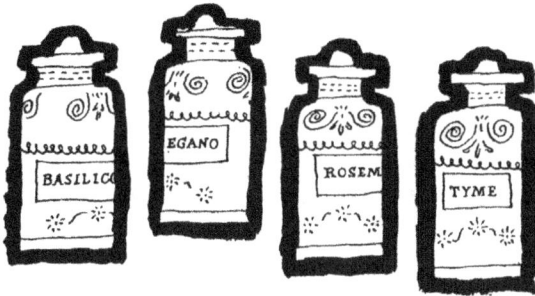

Timballe

Grease well a casserole, line the bottom with a sheet of paper. Place on the paper seven lean slices of bacon spaced in a circle around the edge of the casserole. Prepare the stuffing with breast of veal, a little well-ground lean meat, bread soaked in water well squeezed, Parmesan cheese, eggs, spice, and salt. Make enough stuffing to cover the bottom, the sides and the top of the casserole. After you have lined the casserole, put in the macaroni and cover with the remaining stuffing. Make a coal fire under the casserole and place coals around it. Cover the casserole with an iron lid and place coals on that and let it cook for about an hour. When you are ready to serve it, turn the casserole over on the serving plate and remove the paper which will then be on top. Serve it neatly.

—From Antonio Nebbia's *Il cuoco Maceratese*, second edition, Macerata, MCCCLXXXI.

Spaghetti Dinner

Vermicelli for the Popes

A literary figure of the Renaissance, Platina (1421-1481), who, while living in the Papal Court wrote the Lives of the Roman Pontiffs, took it into his head to contribute to their health by writing a cookbook. Written in Latin, it is one of the oldest in existence. Among his recipes, we find a couple that are not very dissimilar to the modern ones: they tell how to make the actual dough which then could not be purchased in stores, and how to season it with condiments similar to ours except for the use of sugar and spices. On the table of the Popes, spaghetti and macaroni were a dessert rather than an entree, as in America, or a soup, as in Italy.

¶ Eficio sciciliano preparamo in questo modo.
Arina bene buratada e biacha cum chiare di oui aq rosata e comuna bene ipastada.e ridula in pastili onero ffogli subtili come vna paglia.longbi vno somefo distedili.Et qui babi vno stillo di ferro alquo subtile e cauato nelmegio:e cum il capo scauado taglierai sup il foglio:e tueli quel cbe tagli e lassa il resto.Desficata al sole tale vivanda durera p ouo e etiaz ire anni.Maxie se di mese vagosto sara ipastata e... se cu la luna crescete saranno ipastati.Jncl bruodo grasso cocte ...e riducte cu caseo fresco e cu specie dolce debi aspgierle.e po ... di coctura. ¶ Giuanda dicta vermicelli.
Arina prepota come babiano dicto di sopra.e ipastata.riducta i ffogli tagliati in peci a longeza e largeza ouno dedo.e chiamerali vermicell.Al sole bene desficati p ouo ani e piu si coseruerano.Cuocessi p spacio duna boza in bruodo grasso:e i la piadena appebierali cu caso fresco e specie dolce.Et a tepo di vegiuno cuz succo madolino e cu la ete capzino cuocili.ma pcbe il lacte no ricbicde tanta coctura: fali pma buglire alquto in aq :e poi cum la pte di laqua.e azonziui il lacte ecompi di cuocerli.Cocti cuz zucbaro ricozdati di ispargierli. Et tutte vivande di farina vuoleno tale coctura:e no li cuocendo in lacte fali colozidi nel bruodo cum il zaffarano.

Vermicelli for the Popes (from the first Italian translation of Platina's *De honesta voluptate*)

MACARONI SICILIAN STYLE

• Mix well some white flour with the white of an egg, some rose water and some plain water. Make a dough and cut in the form of very fine strips two feet and a half long. With a very fine knitting needle pierce the dough, making a tunnel-like hole. These sausage-looking strips of dough, when dried in the sun, will last two or three years; especially if the dough was kneaded during the full moon of the month of August. Cook them in a rich broth and spread in a pan with grated cheese, freshly churned butter and sweet spices. These "sausages" require two hours of cooking.

> —From Platina (Bartolomeo Sacchi), *De honesta voluptate et valetudine etc.* 1541 ed.

ABOUT VERMICELLI

• Mix the flour as above; when mixed, cut it into little finger-like pieces: you can call them little worms (vermicelli). Expose them to the sun until they are well dried; they will last for two years and more. Put them in a pan and season with grated cheese and spices. But if it happens to be a fast day, you can cook them with the juice of almonds and goat's milk, in which case there is no need of cooking them a long time. Let them boil a short time in water, then add the milk. Do not forget to sprinkle them with sugar when cooked. For all these "sausages" made of flour, the cooking is the same: it is nice to color them with saffron if they were not cooked in milk.

> —From Platina (Bartolomeo Sacchi), *De honesta voluptate et valetudine etc.* 1541 ed.

And Spaghetti for the Presidents

The wheat, in America called durum, which must be used for macaroni products when they are legally manufactured, was known even at the time of the Romans, who cultivated it in Apulia and brought it back home from the Chersonesus (Crimea, Russia). It was then known as wheat with which kings' bread was made. It might be said that durum wheat, made into spaghetti, is suitable not only for kings but also for Presidents of the United States.

Here are three recipes: two of an old and one of a more recent President of the United States: Thomas Jefferson and Franklin D. Roosevelt.

JEFFERSON

I

• Beat 6 eggs until light, add 1 cup milk and ½ teaspoon salt. Add enough flour, about 4 cups, to make a thick dough. Roll, with a rolling pin, to ½-inch thickness. Cut into small pieces and roll these between the hands into long strips resembling macaroni. Cut them to a proper length. Drop into boiling, salted water and cook for 15 minutes. Dress them as you would macaroni. They may also be served boiled in soup.

II

• Break macaroni in small pieces, these should be 2 cupfuls, and boil in salted water until tender. Grate ¼ pound of cheese and mix with the same amount of butter. Stir into the macaroni and bake like *polenta*.

—Through the courtesy of Marie Kimball, author of *Jefferson's Cook Book*, copyright 1938 by Garrett and Massie.

FRANKLIN D. ROOSEVELT
Italian Spaghetti
(Serves 6)

1 lb. spaghetti	½ to 1 pound hamburger
1 large can tomatoes	1 can bouillon or chicken
1 can mushrooms or 6-8	consommé
fresh mushrooms	1 teaspoon salt
4 tablespoons butter	½ teaspoon pepper
1 large finely chopped	2 teaspoons chili powder
onion	

• Sauté onion in part of butter until clear. Add hamburger made into small cakes about size of quarter. When nicely fried, crush and scramble the meat and add mushrooms sautéed in butter and tomatoes. Add bouillon and seasoning and simmer for an hour, or until meat is tender. Serve over 1 lb. of spaghetti which has been boiled and drained. Serve with Parmesan cheese.

—Taken from *The President's Cookbook* by Henrietta Nesbitt. Copyright 1951. Published by Doubleday & Company Inc., New York.

Eleven Kinds of Spaghetti
for Hyphenated Americans

*Spaghetti is now a universal food but the ways of cooking
and seasoning it differ from country to country. Here are
some recipes used by Americans of foreign descent. They
have been suggested by natives of foreign countries or by
editors of American newspapers in foreign languages. Some
were taken from the cookbooks of the foreign countries.*

ARGENTINA

MACARONI

Put in a heat-resistant soup plate half of the macaroni
you cooked, then cover with a layer of all-spiced sausages
(or plain, if you do not have a strong palate), cut in
rounds and fried, then some tomato sauce, and finally the
remaining macaroni. Pour the rest of the sauce over the
macaroni. Sprinkle with cheese (preferably Parmesan) and
place in the oven to make au gratin. Serve it in the same
soup plate.

—From a friend of the author.

BRAZIL

SPAGHETTI NAPOLETANA
(Serves 2)

Cook 8 oz. of spaghetti (a little more than half a pound)
in salted water; stir well. The sauce: cut up 4 oz. of bacon
and 2 large onions into a saucepan and cook over a slow
fire. Add some tomato paste, a spoonful of boiling water,
a spoonful of melted butter and 1 teaspoon of sugar. After
the spaghetti is cooked, strain and add the sauce and serve.

—From Tia Evelina, *Receitas para Você*,
Libr. Josè Olympio editora. Distributed to
visitors at World's Fair, October 1940.

CHINA

FRIED VERMICELLI (Tch'ao mienu)

Add to boiling water ½ pound of vermicelli, remove them, pour water over them and taste them. Clean a bowl full of fresh soft-shelled crabs, fry them in fat and put them aside. Cut 6 ounces of fresh pork into small pieces, fry them as you did the crabs and put aside. Remove the meat from a hard-shelled crab and do as above. Put the vermicelli in 6 ounces of hot fat. When it is of a golden hue, add the preparations above mentioned. Add salt. Before serving, add a little oil, some sesame herb and a little vinegar.

—From L. Lecourt, *La cuisine chinoise*, Pekin 1925.

FRANCE

CROQUETTES PARISIENNE
(Serves 6-8)

1 8-ounce pkg. macaroni	1½ cups milk
4 tablespoons butter	1 egg yolk
6 tablespoons flour	1 egg, beaten
3 tablespoons grated Parmesan cheese	salt
	pepper
1 8-ounce tin marinara sauce	Fat for frying
	Wheat germ

• Boil macaroni according to directions. Drain and chop coarsely.

• Make a thick white sauce with the butter, flour, salt, pepper and milk. Beat in egg yolk and cheese. Mix thoroughly with the chopped macaroni and spread on a large platter to cool.

• Shape into croquettes, roll in flour, dip in beaten egg, roll in wheat germ and fry in deep fat.

• Serve with heated marinara sauce.

—From a Parisian booklet of macaroni recipes.

GERMANY

HAM MACARONI

1 lb. macaroni (cooked, washed and thoroughly cooled)

6 ounces chopped ham, or better, Kasseler Rippchen finely chopped

1½ ounces very fine bacon (Speckstreifen)

1 ounce of butter to grease the mold

¾ cup of sour cream

2 eggs well beaten

½ ounce butter to brown a tablespoon of chopped onion

2 tablespoons very fine chopped mushrooms

1 tablespoon chopped parsley

• In the mold well greased with butter, put 2 or 3 thin slices of bacon, fill with half of the macaroni, complete with the ham and the mixture of onions, mushrooms and parsley. Then add the remaining macaroni, add the eggs which have been well beaten with the cream, put on the remaining pieces of bacon and a little flake of butter. Bake ¾ of an hour in an oven, 350-375 degrees. The sides and upper crust must be very crispy.

—*Personal recipe of Frau Anna (Mrs. Olga Hochstadter), well known food editor of the* Staats-Zeitung und Herold *of New York.*

GREECE

STUFFED "TAGLIATELLE" Greek Style (Kad-neiff)

Boil and season with lard° and good Italian Pecorino
cheese, one pound of tagliatelle which you will place in a
layer about one inch thick in a baking dish, also greased
with lard, and let cool. On the side, prepare the following
seasoning: about ⅓ lb. lean veal, 2 oz. of fat prosciutto
(raw ham), a pinch of chopped parsley, a taste of garlic,
a tablespoon of concentrated meat gravy, 1 oz. bread dough
soaked in milk, the whole thing finely chopped and also
beaten to a pulp, to which necessary salt and pepper will
be added. Cut the layer of cold tagliatelle into lengths
of six inches. Place lengthwise in the center of each strip
a cord-like length of above mixture, folding each strip over
itself lengthwise so as to hold the mixture. Place strips,
so filled, back in the baking dish with the ends under-
neath and brush strips with melted lard, sprinkle with
bread crumbs, again brush with lard, and then place in
hot oven, taking care that each strip be closely placed
together so that heat will not cause them to open. It is
sufficient to bake them for 20 minutes; that is when they
are golden brown. Remove baking dish from oven, let
stand for some time, then cut Kad-neiff crosswise into
small portions.

• Serve on hot dish, cover the Greek Kad-neiff with a
good sauce or meat sauce and grated "caciocavallo" or
Parmesan cheese. Also serve cheese on the side.

                              —From a friend of the author.

°The lamb tail lard or fat used by Greeks may be substituted by
butter or veal kidney fat, melted and made clear.

MEXICO

CHILI CON CREOLE

2 lbs. tripe	1 pinch cayenne
½ lb. ground suet	1 pinch oregano
1 can peas	1 tbsp. molasses
1 can bean sprouts	1 tsp. chili powder
1 chayote	1 chopped onion
1 clove garlic chopped	1 pint water
1 pinch cumin	salt to taste

1 package of macaroni or lasagne or plain broad noodles. Spatter with bits of butter.

• Wash and cut the tripe into 3-inch shoestring strips and place in cold water and bring to a boil. Drain off the boiling water and refill with cold water and bring to boil again and then repeat this process the third time to render the tripe tender but not glutinous. Sauté the ground suet with the chopped onion and the chopped garlic until well browned and then add the cumin (ground comino seeds) and the oregano (Mexican marjoram). Now bring the tripe to a boil with one pint of water and add the suet mixture after the tripe is boiling hot. Boil for full half hour and add the cayenne pepper and salt to taste and boil for 25 minutes more. Pare and cut into sticks the chayote (a pear-like vegetable of the squash family) and add this to the tripe mixture. Add the peas either canned or fresh) and the bean sprouts (either canned or fresh or the cold pack) and boil for 15 minutes. Save the juices of the canned vegetables for thinning the stew later. Add the molasses and boil for five minutes and add the chili powder last and boil an additional 5 minutes. The Chili Con Creole should be tender by this time and if it should be too thick add the vegetable juices. Serve hot on a bed of macaroni or lasagne.

—From a friend of the author.

FISH PUDDING
(Made with wheat germ and macaroni)

2 cups of cooked macaroni	½ cup cream
2 tbsp. melted butter	½ cup fish water
1 tsp. salt	2 eggs, separated
¼ tsp. pepper	cheese
1 lb. fish	

Wheat Germ

• Combine the fish (boiled) with cooked macaroni. Season with salt and pepper. Add cream, fish bouillon, melted butter and egg yolks. Stir the mixture well and fold in the stiffly beaten egg whites. Place in buttered baking dish. Sprinkle generously with grated cheese, dots of butter and wheat germ. Bake 40 minutes. Serve with melted butter.

—From a friend of the author.

MACARONI HUNTER STYLE
(Maccarones à lo cazador)

• Prepare a purée with the meat of a hen, a rabbit and a partridge mixed with some Neapolitan tomato sauce; at the same time cut six truffles into small slices as is done for Julienne soup and add them to the cheese and macaroni. When cooked to their proper crispness, add grated cheese and serve.

—From Adolfo Solichon, *L'arte culinaria*, Madrid, Romo y Füssel [1900].

VENEZUELA
STUFFED GORGUEROS

• Boil cannelloni (gorgueros) in strongly boiling water. Let them drip but not dry. Fill them with a stuffing of chopped ham, or with pieces of sausages mixed with Parmesan cheese and milk. Immerse the cannelloni (gorgueros) in two well-beaten eggs to which some flour has been added. Cook them in strongly boiling olive oil. As they become brown, remove them and place them on some absorbent paper. Sprinkle with grated cheese (parmesan or gruyere) and serve.

—From a friend of the author.

KOSHER RECIPES

MACARONI SALMON FLUFF
(Serves 4)

4 ounces shell macaroni	2 eggs, separated
¼ cup butter or margarine	1 tablespoon minced parsley
3 tablespoons enriched flour	1 cup flaked salmon
2 teaspoons salt	1 cup cooked cut asparagus
2½ cups milk	
2 tablespoons chopped pimiento	

• Cook macaroni in boiling salted water. Drain and rinse. While macaroni is cooking, melt butter or margarine in saucepan. Stir in flour and salt. Gradually add milk and cook until thickened, stirring constantly. Add chopped pimiento. Set aside 1 cup sauce for use as a topping. Add yolks to remaining sauce and blend well. Fold in macaroni, parsley and salmon. Beat egg whites until stiff, but not dry, and fold into macaroni mixture. Pour into greased 8-inch square baking dish and set in pan of hot water. Bake in slow oven (325°F) 1 hour. Add asparagus to sauce which was reserved. Heat and serve over squares of Macaroni Salmon Fluff.

—Through the courtesy of
Miss Joan E. Thimm.

CORONATION MUSHROOMS

1 lb. fresh mushrooms, large
½ cup bread crumbs
¼ cup defatted wheat germ
½ cup grated Parmesan cheese

½ lb. wagon wheels
1 can Marinara Sauce
salt
pepper
mozzarella cheese

• Remove stems from mushrooms. Place mushroom caps in baking pan which has been greased with olive oil or butter. Mix bread crumbs, wheat germ, and Parmesan cheese and salt and pepper to taste and put about a tablespoonful on each mushroom. Parboil wagon wheels according to package directions. Drain and place 2 wheels in center of each mushroom (on top of each other). In each opening of wheels place a small piece of mozzarella cheese. Garnish each mushroom with about 1 tbsp. marinara sauce. Bake for 12-20 minutes in moderate oven.

—Through the courtesy of
Miss Joan E. Thimm.

BAKED STUFFED GREEN PEPPERS

6 medium-sized green
  peppers
¼ cup minced onion
¾ cup sliced mushrooms
¼ cup butter or margarine
¼ cup flour
½ teaspoon salt
Few grains pepper

2 cups milk
½ 8-oz. pkg. elbow
  macaroni
1 7-oz. can (1 cup) tuna,
  flaked
1 cup grated American
  cheddar cheese.

Wash green peppers; cut slice from stem end; remove seeds. Cover peppers with boiling salted water; boil uncovered, 3-5 minutes; drain. Sauté onion and mushrooms in butter or margarine until tender; blend in flour, salt and pepper; gradually add milk, cook, stirring constantly, until thickened. Cook and drain macaroni, according to directions on package. Combine sauce; macaroni, tuna and ½ cup cheese. Stuff peppers with macaroni mixture. Sprinkle tops with remaining cheese. Place in baking pan; bake in moderate oven, 325°F., about 30 minutes. Yields 6 servings.

—Through the courtesy of
Miss Joan E. Thimm.

Four Ways of Preparing Spaghetti in Accordance with the Tastes of Calabria, Genoa, Rome and Sicily

Italians who came to this country brought with them their own methods of cooking. Later dietitians recognized the values of Italian recipes. These are the heritage of long experience and reflect the taste of an artistic race. The contribution of Italians to America in the field of food is not inferior to that in the realm of thought and in the arts.

REGIONAL ITALIAN RECIPES

ANCHOVY SAUCE CALABRESE STYLE

Ingredients: a clove of garlic, about 2 oz. salted anchovies or half a tube of anchovy paste; two tablespoons olive oil; two tablespoons bread crumbs dried in oven for a few minutes.

• Cook spaghetti in the usual manner for 15 minutes. Meanwhile, heat oil in frying pan together with garlic clove slightly crushed. As soon as oil is hot, remove garlic and add anchovy paste or salted anchovies (washed and boned). Stir, let cook for a few minutes, and add bread crumbs. Mix well with wooden spoon and pour cooked spaghetti into this mixture after having drained it. Mix and place in serving dish. This sauce does not require any grated cheese.

> —Through the courtesy of A. Mondadori, publishers of the weekly *Grazia*.

GENOESE "PESTO"

Ingredients: 4 garlic cloves; two handfuls of basil leaves; two tablespoons of shelled pine cone nuts (pignoli); a tablespoon salt; about 1 oz. sharp pecorino or Sardinian cheese; half a glass of oil.

• Cook lasagne in abundant salted water and prepare the sauce by chopping finely the garlic, washed basil leaves and salt. Place this in a mortar and crush thoroughly. When ingredients are well amalgamated, add pine cone nuts and, little by little, half of the grated cheese. Crush and mix well, add oil slowly so as to give the mixture a cream-like consistency. When ready to serve, add two or three tablespoons of boiling water—using preferably the water in which macaroni was cooked—then drain lasagne, season with "pesto" and sprinkle with remaining cheese.

    —Through the courtesy of A. Mondadori,
    publishers of the weekly *Grazia*.

SAUCE ROMAN STYLE

Ingredients: about 2 oz. tuna fish in olive oil; one clove garlic; two tablespoons tomato sauce; a teaspoon oregano seeds; one tablespoon oil; a pinch of pepper.

• Crush garlic clove slightly and place in a small frying pan with oil; as soon as garlic begins to brown, remove it and put in its place the tuna fish not too finely chopped. Let cook for a few minutes; then add tomato sauce diluted with a little hot water; add pepper, crush tuna fish with a wooden spoon, mix and let cook for a few minutes. At last moment add oregano seeds, bring to a boil and season macaroni with this sauce after having cooked it in the usual way.

    —Through the courtesy of A. Mondadori,
    publishers of the weekly *Grazia*.

FUSILLI (Twists) with Cauliflower
Sicilian Style

1 lb. fusilli (pasta)   1 tbsp. pignoli (pine nuts)
1 small cauliflower   1 tbsp. currants
1 large diced onion   3 filets of anchovy
1 No. 2 can tomatoes   Salt and pepper to taste
4 tbsp. olive oil

• Wash and break or cut cauliflower into small pieces. Cook in rapidly boiling salted water about 12 minutes or until tender but not soft. Drain; set aside.
• Heat oil in saucepan; add onion; cook 3 minutes or until soft. Cut up anchovies; add; stir about 2 minutes or until dissolved. Add tomatoes; cover; simmer 20 minutes. Add cauliflower, pine nuts, currants, and very little salt and pepper. Mix well; keep hot over very low flame.
• Cook fusilli in 4 quarts of rapidly boiling salted water 15 minutes or until tender. Drain; place in hot bowl; add cauliflower and sauce.
• Serve very hot in individual plates. (If desired, Fusilli with Cauliflower may be sprinkled with grated Romano cheese just before serving.)

—Through the courtesy of Maria Lo Pinto, author of *The Art of Italian Cooking*, New York, Doubleday & Co. Inc., 1950.

Recipes by the Food Editors
of American Newspapers

Food editors of the important newspapers and magazines in the United States could hardly overlook as popular a dish as spaghetti. For many years, they have offered recipes adapted to the most varied tastes. A history of the mounting popularity of this Italian dish might be written by noting the increasing number of recipes published in the press. Four contributions by as many leading food editors in the press of New York are used here, with grateful acknowledgment of their kindness in granting permission to reprint them.

JIFFY MACARONI AND CHEESE
(Serves 4-6)

1 tbsp. salt
3 qts. boiling water
8 oz. elbow macaroni
1 small onion, grated
1 can condensed cream of
    chicken or mushroom
    soup

¼ tsp. rich-prepared
    mustard
Salt and pepper
1 cup grated cheddar
    cheese
2 medium-sized tomatoes
¼ cup grated cheddar
    cheese

• Add 1 tbsp. salt to rapidly boiling water. Gradually add macaroni so that water continues to boil. Cook uncovered, stirring occasionally, until tender.
• Drain in colander. Combine macaroni and grated onion. Turn into a greased 1½-qt. casserole. Heat oven to 350°F. (moderate).
• In a saucepan, heat soup thoroughly; add mustard, salt and pepper to taste, and 1 cup cheese, stirring until

cheese melts. Remove from heat and pour sauce over
macaroni in casserole. Slice tomatoes ½″ thick and place
slices in a circle on macaroni mixture. Sprinkle remaining
¼ cup cheese over tomato slices.

• Bake at 350° F. 25 to 30 min. or until lightly browned.
    —Through the courtesy of *The American Weekly*,
    March 23, 1952, Miss Amy Alden, Food Editor.

SPAGHETTI BEEF CASSEROLE
(Serves 4-6)

1 tbsp. salt	1 6-oz. can tomato paste
3 qts. boiling water	⅛ tsp. paprika
8 oz. spaghetti	$1/_{16}$ tsp. cayenne pepper
1 tbsp. fat	½ tsp. salt
⅓ cup finely chopped	½ tsp. Worcestershire sauce
onion	¼ tsp. Tabasco sauce
¾ lb. chuck beef, ground	¾ cup grated processed
1 No. 2 can tomatoes	American cheddar
(2½ cups)	cheese

• Heat oven to 350° F. (moderate). Add 1 tbsp. salt to
rapidly boiling water. Gradually add spaghetti so that
water continues to boil. Cook, uncovered, stirring occasionally, until almost tender. Drain in colander. Melt fat in a
heavy skillet; add onion and beef; sauté until tender.
Thoroughly stir in tomatoes, tomato paste and all ingredients except cheese. Combine spaghetti, meat mixture
and cheese; mix lightly. Turn into a greased 1½-qt. casserole and bake at 350° F. 20 to 30 min.
• If preferred, elbow macaroni may be used in place of
spaghetti.
    —Through the courtesy of *The American Weekly*,
    March 23, 1952, Miss Amy Alden, Food Editor.

SPAGHETTI TETRAZZINI
(Serves 6)

¼ cup butter or margarine
3 tbsps. flour
3 drops yellow coloring
1 pt. light cream
1 tsp. salt
1½-lb. chicken,°cooked
2 tbsps. salt

4 qts. boiling water
1 lb. thin spaghetti
¼ cup butter or margarine
2 tbsps. grated Italian
  cheese
Additional grated
  Italian cheese

Dash of paprika

• In a saucepan melt ¼ cup butter over low heat. Add flour and blend. Add coloring and cream; simmer until thick, stirring constantly. Stir in 1 tsp. salt. Chop dark chicken meat. Add to half of cream sauce. Add 2 tbsps. salt to rapidly boiling water. Gradually add spaghetti so that water continues to boil. Cook uncovered, stirring occasionally, until tender. Drain in colander. Add ¼ cup margarine and 2 tbsps. cheese. Combine with chicken-cream sauce. Slice breast of chicken paper-thin. In individual casseroles, place spaghetti mixture; top with slice of chicken breast. Spread with cream sauce. Sprinkle with cheese and dash of paprika. Place under broiler until golden brown. Serve immediately.

—Through the courtesy of *The American Weekly*,
March 23, 1952, Miss Amy Alden, Food Editor.

°2½ cups canned boned turkey can be used in place of cooked chicken.

EGG NOODLES WITH SWEDISH MEAT BALLS
(Serves 6)

The Noodles:

1 tbsp. salt
3 qts. boiling water
8 oz. cooked noodles
¼ cup finely minced onion

2 tbsps. butter or
  margarine
½ cup hot cooked spinach,
  finely chopped

• Add salt to rapidly boiling water. Gradually add egg noodles so that water continues to boil. Cook, uncovered, stirring occasionally, until tender. Drain in colander. While noodles are cooking, sauté minced onion in butter or margarine. Add hot spinach and toss with hot noodles. Season to taste with salt and pepper. Serve with Swedish Meat Balls.

Swedish Meat Balls:

1 cup bread crumbs
⅓ cup milk
¼ cup minced onion
1 lb. chuck beef, ground
1 egg, slightly beaten
1 tsp. salt
⅛ tsp. pepper

¼ tsp. nutmeg
2 tbsps. butter or
  margarine
2 tbsps. flour
1½ cups beef bouillon°
⅓ cup light cream

• Soak bread crumbs in milk; mix with onion, meat, egg, salt, pepper and nutmeg. Mix lightly but thoroughly. Shape into small balls (allow 3 per serving) and sauté in butter until lightly browned. Remove meat balls. Blend flour with drippings in skillet. Gradually add bouillon and cream and stir until mixture thickens. Return meat balls to gravy, cover and simmer 15 minutes.

> —Through the courtesy of *The American Weekly*, March 23, 1952, Miss Amy Alden, Food Editor.

°Use canned or that made from meat or vegetable extract paste or cubes.

MACARONI BACON CASSEROLE
(Serves 4-6)

1 tbsp. salt	½ tsp. caraway seeds
3 qts. boiling water	½ tsp. salt
8 oz. elbow macaroni	⅛ tsp. black pepper
2 cans condensed tomato soup, undiluted	1 cup grated cheddar cheese
1 cup sliced, peeled onions	4 strips bacon

• Heat oven to 400° F. Add salt to rapidly boiling water. Gradually add macaroni so that water continues to boil. Cook, uncovered, stirring occasionally, until tender. Drain in colander. In a large bowl combine soup, onions, seasonings and cheese; mix well. Add cooked macaroni; mix lightly. Place mixture in a greased 1½-qt. baking dish. Top with bacon strips. Bake in 400° F. oven 25 min. Serve immediately.

—Through the courtesy of *The American Weekly*, March 23, 1952, Miss Amy Alden, Food Editor.

SALMON SPAGHETTI
(Serves 4-6)

1 tbsp. salt	¼ cup melted butter or margarine
3 qts. boiling water	
8 oz. thin spaghetti	½ cup sliced stuffed olives
1 12-oz. can cream of celery soup	¼ tsp. sweet basil
	⅛ tsp. black pepper
¾ cup milk	1 tsp. onion salt

1 1-lb. can salmon, drained

• Add 1 tbsp. salt to rapidly boiling water. Cook spaghetti, uncovered, in boiling water, stirring occasionally, until just tender. Drain. Mix remaining ingredients in large bowl, adding spaghetti last. Stir gently with fork. Pour into greased 1½-qt. casserole; cover and bake in oven of 350° F. for 30 min.

—Through the courtesy of *The American Weekly,* March 23, 1952, Miss Amy Alden, Food Editor.

FAVORITE SPAGHETTI

4 ounces long spaghetti
2 tablespoons cooking oil or bacon drippings
2 tablespoons chopped parsley
2 tablespoons chopped onion
1 clove garlic, sliced
½ pound ground beef

2½ cups cooked tomatoes (No. 2 can)
1 cup tomato sauce (8-ounce can)
1 tablespoon of Worcestershire sauce
¼ cup mushrooms (optional)
¼ cup grated Parmesan cheese

• Cook spaghetti in boiling salted water until tender (about 10 minutes). Drain. While spaghetti is cooking, heat oil in skillet. Add parsley, onion and garlic and brown lightly. Add beef and cook until brown. Add tomatoes, tomato sauce, Worcestershire sauce and mushrooms. Cover and cook slowly until thick (about 45 minutes). Sprinkle with cheese before serving.
• An attractive way to serve pasta is in loaf form. Cut it at table and serve with tomato, cheese, mushroom or fish sauce.

—Through the courtesy of Eleanor Richey Johnston, and the *Christian Science Monitor* of January 2, 1953

MACARONI ASPIC
(Serves 6)

2¼ cups tomato juice
  (No. 2 can)
1 bay leaf
1 large piece celery
Dash paprika
2 tablespoons tarragon
  vinegar

2 slices onion
2 ounces shell macaroni
1 tablespoon gelatin
¼ cup cold water
12 cooked asparagus spears
  (No. 2 can)

• Combine first 6 ingredients in 2-quart saucepan. Bring to boiling point. Add macaroni. Cook 15 minutes. Remove bay leaf, celery and onion. Soften gelatin in water. Add to hot mixture. Stir until dissolved. When mixture begins to thicken, pour into rectangular 6x8-inch mold or individual molds in which asparagus spears have been arranged. Chill.
• If you like pasta in salad, try putting it in a tomato aspic for a new salad treat.

> —Through the courtesy of Eleanor Richey Johnston, and the *Christian Science Monitor* of January 2, 1953

MACARONI LOAF
(Serves 6)

1 cup macaroni broken in 2-inch pieces
½ pound American cheese
1½ cups hot milk
1 cup soft bread crumbs
¼ cup melted butter or margarine
1 pimiento, chopped

1 tablespoon each, chopped onion and chopped parsley
Salt, pepper and paprika
3 eggs, beaten
Tomato sauce
Parsley for garnish

• Cook macaroni in boiling salted water. Drain and blanch with cold water. Melt cheese in top of double boiler. Add milk gradually, stirring constantly. Remove from heat and add crumbs, butter, pimiento, chopped parsley and onion; season to taste. Add eggs and fold in the macaroni. Pour into well-greased loaf pan and bake about 50 minutes, or until firm, at 325°F. Unmold and serve with tomato sauce. Garnish with parsley.

—Through the courtesy of Eleanor Richey Johnston, and the *Christian Science Monitor* of January 2, 1953

EGG MACARONI SALAD
(Serves 4)

1 pkg. (8 oz.) elbow
macaroni
3 quarts boiling water
3 teaspoons salt
Cooking time: Fifteen
minutes, or until tender
⅓ cup mayonnaise (about)
2 teaspoons prepared
mustard
½ teaspoon salt, or more
⅛ teaspoon pepper

½ cup sliced celery
2 tablespoons chopped
parsley
4 hard-cooked eggs,
quartered
2 ripe tomatoes, cut into
wedges
Chilling time: Twenty
minutes
Salad greens

• Cook the macaroni rapidly in the boiling salted water
in an uncovered kettle until tender, stirring occasionally.
Drain in a colander; rinse with cold water; drain. Cool.
Turn into a salad bowl; separate with a fork.
• Combine the mayonnaise, mustard, remaining salt,
pepper, celery and parsley. Mix into the macaroni. Add
the eggs and tomato and mix lightly. Chill. Decorate the
bowl with lettuce or other salad greens, tucked between
the bowl and the salad. Garnish with mayonnaise and
serve.

—Through the courtesy of the *New York
Daily News*, Nancy Dorris, Food Editor,
May 17, 1952

MACARONI SALAD
(Serves 4-6)

1 pkg. (8 oz.) elbow macaroni

2 cups diced cooked chicken, ham, veal, shrimp, tuna, or salmon

1 cup chopped celery or cabbage

½ cup French dressing

1 tablespoon grated onion

1 teaspoon salt (about)

⅛ teaspoon pepper

Chilling time:Twenty minutes

¼ cup chopped green pepper or canned pimiento

½ cup mayonnaise or salad dressing (about)

Salad greens

• Drain the cooked macaroni; rinse in cold water; drain; cool. Combine the chicken, meat or fish, celery and mixed French dressing, onion, salt and pepper in a salad bowl; chill. Separate the macaroni with a fork and add to the salad with the peppers and mayonnaise. Mix lightly. Garnish with salad greens and serve with assorted appetizers and seed rolls.

—Through the courtesy of the *New York Daily News*, Nancy Dorris, Food Editor, May 17, 1952

LASAGNE AL FORNO
(Serves 6)

2 tablespoons olive oil	1 box enriched curly edge
1 pound ground beef (or	Lasagne
½ pound beef plus ½	5 quarts water
pound pork)	3 tablespoons salt
1 medium onion, minced	1 pound thinly sliced
1 clove garlic	mozzarella cheese
½ can tomato paste	3 tablespoons grated
2 cups water	Italian-type cheese

• Put the olive oil in a frying pan. In it brown the meat, onion and garlic. Combine tomato paste, water and salt and pepper to taste. Pour over the browned meat. Let simmer slowly for 1½ hours.

• Bring the five quarts of water to a boil, add 3 tablespoons salt and gently place Lasagne, one piece at a time, into the boiling water.

• Cook for 15 minutes, stirring occasionally. Drain Lasagne immediately it is cooked.

• In a casserole arrange a layer of cooked Lasagne, a layer of meat sauce and a layer of sliced mozzarella cheese. Repeat until Lasagne is used. (Save enough of the meat sauce to pour over the finished dish).

• Top casserole with the grated cheese. Bake at 375 degrees for about 20 minutes.

—Through the courtesy of the *New York Journal American*, Janet Cook, Food Editor, April 9, 1952

Just for Laughs
and to show the great change
in American cooking,
we submit a recipe of 1823

MACCARONI

• The usual mode of dressing it in this country is by adding a white sauce, and Parmesan or Cheshire cheese and burning it(!); but this makes a dish which is proverbially unwholesome; but its bad qualities arise from the oiled and burnt cheese, and the half dressed flour and butter put into the white sauce.

• Maccaroni plain boiled, and some rich stock or potable soup added to it quite hot, in deep tureen, and let each guest add grated Parmesan and cold butter, or oiled[?] butter served hot, and it is excellent; this is the most common Italian mode of dressing it. Maccaroni, with cream, sugar, and Cinnamon, or a little *Varicelli* added to the Cream, makes a very nice sweet dish.

—From John Armstrong's *The Cook's Oracle containing recipes for plain cookery*, Boston, 1823. 2nd American edition.

Recipes from the Best
American Cook Books and
Some Italian Recipes

American publishers and editors of cook books almost universally recognize the importance of a spaghetti dish to the American menu. Of five hundred American cook books that are available at the present time, ninety per cent include at least one recipe; in many cases several. American taste has transformed this food, a century ago considered foreign, into one of the most popular dishes on the American table. Some recipes from the best current cook books are here presented with grateful acknowledgment.

QUICK MACARONI ANTIPASTO

1 can Raviolettes
½ 8-ounce package Shells
1 tin minced ham
1 jar prepared cheese
 spread

artichoke hearts in oil
olives
celery hearts
salami
tomatoes

• Cook and drain shells according to directions; stuff half with minced ham and half with cheese. Heat raviolettes and spear each one with a toothpick. Arrange with other antipasto ingredients on a large dish.

—Originated by Mrs. Letizia Buitoni

SPAGHETTI CASSEROLES
(Serves 6)

1 cup chopped onion
1 garlic clove, chopped
½ cup sliced, canned or
 fresh mushrooms
3 tablespoons fat or salad
 oil
¾ lb. chopped beef
1 teaspoon salt
1 tablespoon sugar
Few grains pepper

3 8-oz. cans mushroom
 sauce
1 8-oz. package 20% protein
 spaghetti
1 2½-oz. jar grated Parmesan cheese
1 cup defatted wheat germ
¼ cup melted butter or
 margarine

• Brown onion lightly with garlic and mushrooms in fat or oil; add meat; brown slightly. Add salt, sugar, pepper and mushroom sauce. Cook and drain spaghetti according to directions on package. Arrange spaghetti, sauce and cheese in alternate layers in casserole. Toss together wheat germ and butter, and sprinkle over spaghetti. Bake in moderately hot oven (375°F.), 30 minutes.

—Italian recipe

TOMATO SAUSAGE CASSEROLE
(Serves 6)

2-8 oz. cans Ragù Sauce	Few grains pepper
1¼ cups hot water	Pinch of oregano
1-8 oz. pkg. large macaroni	1½ lbs. sausage meat
1 large onion, sliced	½ cup grated Parmesan
½ teaspoon salt	cheese

• Combine sauce and water; bring to boiling point. Add uncooked macaroni; cover; let stand while preparing rest of ingredients. Add onion, salt, pepper and oregano. Pour into 1½ quart casserole; cover. Bake in moderate oven, 350°F. for ½ hour. Form sausage into flat cakes; sauté; turning to brown both sides. Place well-drained sausage cakes on macaroni; sprinkle with cheese. Bake uncovered ½ hour.

—Old Italian recipe

SPAGHETTI SICILIAN STYLE

1 lb. spaghetti	½ cup Parmesan cheese
1 doz. filets of anchovy	grated
½ cup olive oil	Salt and pepper
1 small clove garlic	

• Fry garlic in oil until brown. Remove garlic and cut anchovies into small pieces, add to oil and cook about 2 minutes. Add pepper and small pinch of salt. Cook spaghetti in boiling salted water until tender. Drain and pour sauce over it. Top with cheese if so desired.

by SIGNOR ANGELO DI BELLA, *Manager of El Borracho*
—From *Love and Dishes* by Nicolo de Quattrociocchi, Copyright 1950. Published by Bobbs Merrill Company, Inc., Indianapolis.

SPAGHETTI OR MACARONI IN CREAM

• Cook 1 lb. spaghetti, macaroni or noodles in boiling salted water 15 to 18 minutes. If preferred underdone, cook 10 to 12 minutes. Melt some butter in a saucepan and add the well-drained spaghetti, macaroni or noodles. Season with salt and pepper, and mix in some grated Parmesan or Swiss cheese and butter. Drain and place in a saucepan with some butter. Add enough cream to cover the spaghetti. Cook until reduced to half its original quantity and thicken with a little cream or Béchamel sauce and grated Parmesan cheese.

> —From *Cooking a la Ritz* by Louis Diat. Copyright 1941. Published by J.B.Lippincott Company, Philadelphia.

ITALIAN SPAGHETTI

1½ lbs. ground round steak
1 medium can mushrooms
½ green pepper, chopped
2 medium onions, chopped
Garlic to taste

1 small bottle (2 oz.) olive oil
1 No. 2 can tomatoes
1 small can tomato purée

• Sauté meat, mushrooms, pepper, onions and garlic in olive oil. Add tomatoes and purée. Let simmer for 1 hour. Serve over spaghetti that has been cooked in salt water. Serve with grated Parmesan cheese.

> —From *The American Hostess,* by Ida Lee Dunne. Copyright 1948. Published by Dunne Press, Louisville.

ITALIAN SPAGHETTI

• While the spaghetti is cooking—about 2 cups per serving—make the sauce. Mince 1 clove of garlic; add to 1 tablespoon olive oil, and fry lightly for five minutes until brown. Add ½ cup condensed tomato soup or prepared tomato sauce, salt, pepper, and a pinch of dried basil, and cook gently for 5 minutes. Keep hot until the spaghetti is ready. Put the spaghetti on a hot plate, pour the sauce on top and add lots of grated Parmesan cheese. The basic sauce can be varied by adding chopped mushrooms or chicken livers or both, sautéed separately in a little butter. Place them on top of the sauce before adding the cheese.

—From *Cooking for One* by Eleanor Parker. Copyright 1946. Published by Thomas Y. Crowell, New York.

SPAGHETTI WITH MEAT BALLS
(4 servings)

½ pound ground meat	¼ cup olive oil
½ teaspoon salt	1 can tomato paste
¼ teaspoon pepper	1½ cups water
1 large onion, chopped	½ bay leaf
1 clove garlic	½ pound spaghetti
¼ pound mushrooms, sliced	grated cheese

• Shape the salted and peppered meat into balls the size of large marbles. Cook the meat, mushrooms, onion and garlic in the oil over low heat until the onion is yellow; add the tomato paste, water, and seasonings. Simmer until thick. Remove the bay leaf and the garlic. Boil the spaghetti and put on a large hot platter; arrange the meat balls around the spaghetti; pour the sauce over. Pass grated cheese.

—From *The Basic Cookbook* by Marjorie Heseltine and Ula M. Dow. Copyright 1941. Published by Houghton Mifflin Company, Boston.

MEAT ROLLS AND SPAGHETTI SAUCE

• For the rolls you will need 4 slabs of round steak cut ¼ inch thick, each weighing ½ pound or a little more. The slabs should be as nearly oblong as possible and the meat should be solid. If you let your butcher know ahead of time just what you want, he can save you exactly the right cuts. After the meat is cut, ask the butcher to cover the pieces with heavy paper and pound them flat, as for Wiener Schnitzel or scallopini. When pounded, the pieces should be approximately 5 inches wide and 10 inches long. Lay the slabs on a board, cut away fat if there is any and spread a little finely minced garlic over each. I use 1 medium clove garlic for each piece—and that's quite some garlic. If you're a little standoffish about garlic, use less.
• Now the stuffing for the rolls. Crumble 7 slices white bread into a bowl and add ¼ cup chopped parsley, ½ cup grated Parmesan cheese, 5 tablespoons finely chopped onion, 6 tablespoons olive oil, 1 teaspoon salt, ½ teaspoon freshly ground black pepper, 1 teaspoon dried sweet basil and ¼ cup cold water.

Blend thoroughly and taste for seasoning. Have 4 hard-boiled eggs and some canned pimiento at hand and you're ready to make the rolls.
• Divide stuffing equally among the 4 meat slabs and put it down firmly over entire surface. Cover each with thin

slices of hard-boiled eggs. Cut pimiento into thin strips and put 8 or 10 strips on each slab. Now roll firmly, beginning at narrow end, and fasten with toothpicks all around so that the stuffing won't leak out during cooking. Put some olive oil in a skillet, and when hot add meat rolls and let them brown delicately on all sides. Don't let them form a crust, or you'll have trouble when you slice them. Put browned rolls in the bottom of a large earthenware casserole or a heavy saucepan.

• Put 3 or 4 finely minced cloves garlic and 1 Spanish onion, chopped, in the skillet in which you browned the meat, and when delicately browned add 3 cups tomato purée, 1 small can concentrated tomato paste, 2 cups water, 1 tablespoon salt, 1 tablespoon sugar, ¼ teaspoon freshly ground black pepper, 1 large green pepper, chopped, 5 tablespoons chopped parsley, and 1 or more cans button mushrooms, liquid and all. The mushrooms can be omitted, but they're a mighty nice addition. Stir occasionally, but be careful not to jab the spoon into the meat rolls. You'll have to add a little water during the cooking unless your utensil has a tight-enough lid to prevent evaporation. When cooking time is almost over, do a good job of tasting and add more of any seasoning you think is needed. This is the sauce for your spaghetti and it should be energetic.

• The meat and sauce can be cooked the day before and reheated before serving. I've done it that way and it's very good, but not quite so good as if it is cooked the day of the party—and really, that's so easy to do. Make meat rolls the day before. Have all ingredients for the sauce measured, chopped and mixed, except for onions and garlic. It will take only about 20 minutes to brown meat, garlic and onion, heat the sauce and put the whole business on to cook.

• Use a large saucepan of heavily salted boiling water for

the spaghetti. Cooking time will vary slightly for different brands and for different sizes of spaghetti. After 10 or 11 minutes, remove a strand and taste it. When done, the spaghetti should be chewy, not soft—*al dente* is the idea. Drain, pour boiling water over it and drain again. Return spaghetti to kettle in which it was cooked and ladle a lot, but by no means all, of the sauce over it. Toss with two large forks until each strand is coated with sauce. Remove toothpicks from meat rolls, and with a very sharp thin-bladed knife, cut across into 1-inch slices. The slices will look like pin wheels and they'll taste even better than they look. Turn spaghetti onto a platter, sprinkle with grated Parmesan cheese and ladle on some more sauce. Make a border of meat-roll slices and garnish with parsley. Pour the rest of the sauce into a bowl and serve it and a bowl of grated Parmesan cheese with the spaghetti.

> —From *Cooking For Company* by Ruth Mills Teague. Copyright 1950. Published by Random House, New York.

CLAM SPAGHETTINI A LA MARINARA
(Serves 4-6)

1 clove garlic	1 8-ounce package
1 tablespoon olive oil	spaghettini
1 can minced clams	salt
1 can marinara sauce	pepper

• Halve garlic and brown it in the oil; then remove the garlic. To the oil add the clams, including the juice, the marinara sauce, and the seasoning. Allow to simmer over low flame while cooking the spaghettini according to directions. When the spaghettini are drained (it is not

necessary to shake the colander while draining spaghettini)
pour the hot sauce over them and serve immediately.
• VARIATIONS: 1. Increase the amount of olive oil and
omit the marinara sauce for a different taste sensation.
2. Add sautéd onions to either recipe.
—Adapted by Mrs. Letizia Buitoni.

SPAGHETTI SAUCES

OIL AND GARLIC SAUCE

⅔ cup fine olive oil   Fresh or dried sweet basil
3 cloves garlic   1 teaspoon salt

• Heat olive oil with garlic cloves, which have been
peeled and slightly crushed with a heavy-bladed knife
or a wooden spoon. Add basil to taste, and salt. Press
garlic cloves several times while the oil is heating, so that
the essence of the garlic will distribute itself.
• Arrange spaghetti on plates and add the garlic-flavored
oil and basil—and bits of garlic as well, if desired. Sprinkle
with freshly ground black pepper and a generous amount
of freshly grated Parmesan cheese.
—From the *Fireside Cook Book* by
James A. Beard. Copyright 1949. Published by Simon and Schuster, Inc., New
York.

CRAB SAUCE FOR SPAGHETTI
(Serves 6-7)

½ cup thinly sliced onions
1 tbsp. minced parsley
1 tbsp. chopped celery
4 tbsp. olive oil
1 cup well drained canned
  or fresh tomatoes

1½ cups water
Salt, pepper, ½ tsp. paprika
1 lb. crab meat
¼ cup sherry
1 lb. spaghetti
grated cheese

• Cook the onions, parsley, and celery in the olive oil until lightly browned, using a large saucepan. Add the tomatoes, plenty of salt and black pepper, and paprika. Simmer for about 1 hour, slowly adding water; longer will not matter. Add the crab meat—well picked over for shell— and the sherry. Simmer until piping hot. In the meantime, cook the spaghetti until tender. Drain and put on a large platter and cover with sauce, mixing them together well. Either put the cheese right over the spaghetti or pass it separately. Serve immediately.

> —From *How To Cook Well* by Ann Roe Robbins. Copyright 1946. Published by Thomas Y. Crowell, New York

SPAGHETTI GREEN SAUCE
(25 minutes, serves 2)

• Brown 4 minced garlic cloves in ½ cup salad oil. Add 1 cup chopped parsley. Simmer 5 minutes. Season with black pepper. Serve over boiled spaghetti with lots of grated cheese.

> —From *The Glamour Magazine After Five Cookbook* by Beverly Pepper. Copyright 1952. Published by Doubleday and Company, Inc., New York.

SPAGHETTI SAUCE
(Serves 4)

• Chop together and place in a casserole, 2 medium-sized onions, 1 clove of garlic, and a couple of sprigs of parsley. Cook in olive oil with mixed herbs until soft but not brown. Add 1 can of condensed tomato soup and 1 can of water in which a bouillon cube has been dissolved. Add salt to taste, black pepper and more herbs if desired. Brown very small bits of ground beef in butter and add. I do not give the amount of ground meat because that depends on whether you want a very meaty sauce or not. I use about ¾ pound because we like lots of meat. Brown ½ pound of mushrooms in butter and add. The longer the sauce simmers, the better it is.

—From *When The Cook's Away* by Peggy Harvey. Copyright 1952. Published by Henry Regnery Company, Chicago.

GREEN TAGLIATELLE

CHICKEN LIVER CASSEROLE
(Serves 4-6)

1 8-oz. package Tagliatelle *Verdi* (green medium ribbons)
1 lb. chicken livers
2 tablespoons flour, seasoned
½ cup butter or margarine
½ cup chopped onion
1 garlic clove, chopped

1 No. 2½ can tomatoes
1 6-oz. can tomato paste
1 4-oz. can mushrooms
2 tablespoons sugar
1 teaspoon salt
few grains pepper
1 2½-oz. jar Parmesan cheese
1 cup soft bread crumbs

• Cook and drain green tagliatelle according to directions on package. Roll chicken livers in seasoned flour; sauté in ¼ cup butter or margarine with onion and garlic, until golden brown. Add tomatoes, tomato paste, mushrooms, sugar, salt and pepper. Bring to boiling point and add tagliatelle and cheese. Pour into greased casserole. Melt remaining ¼ cup butter; add crumbs. Sprinkle crumbs on mixture in casserole. Bake in moderate oven (375°F.) for 35 minutes.

SPAGHETTI ALLA TEDESCA

1 No. 2 can tomatoes
¼ teaspoon baking soda
3 tablespoons butter
4 tablespoons flour
1 teaspoon salt
1 teaspoon Worcestershire
  sauce
½ to 1 teaspoon garlic salt
⅛ teaspoon cayenne
¼ teaspoon oregano

1½ cups milk
⅓ cup ale
½ lb. sharp American
  cheddar cheese, broken
  in pieces
⅓ cup Chianti
¼ cup chopped olives
1 lb. Tagliatelle Verdi
  (green medium ribbons)

• Drain juice from canned tomatoes, break tomatoes in small pieces; add soda and mix well. Melt butter; blend in flour, salt, Worcestershire sauce, garlic salt, cayenne and oregano. Add milk; cook, stirring constantly, until thick. Add tomatoes, ale and cheese; cook, stirring constantly until cheese is melted. Add chianti and chives. Keep hot. Cook tagliatelle according to directions on package. Drain well. Place on serving dish; cover with sauce. Serve immediately.
• VARIATION: Add 1 jar (2½ oz.) dried beef to sauce.

—Italian recipe

TAGLIATELLE VERDI AU GRATIN

• In a baking dish alternate layers of cooked tagliatelle (with salt and pepper) and grated American cheese. Pour on a cup of warm milk, then add dices of buttered bread and sprinkle with cheese. Bake in moderate (375°F.) oven until golden brown. Serve hot.

—Italian recipe

MACARONI

LOBSTER AND MACARONI AU GRATIN
(Serves 3-4)

1 (½ pound) can lobster   3 tablespoons fine dry
3 tablespoons dry sherry   bread crumbs
1 can macaroni and cheese   2 tablespoons melted
                                        butter

•   Dice the lobster and add the sherry.
•   Arrange in layers with the macaroni in individual baking dishes; make the first and last layers of the macaroni.
•   Cover with the crumbs moistened with the butter; bake about 25 minutes, or until bubbling, in a moderate oven (375°F.).

> —From *Food For Two* by Ida Bailey Allen. Copyright 1947. Published by the Garden City Publishing Company, New York.

BAKED MACARONI WITH CHEESE

1 (8 ounce) package   1½ cups milk
   macaroni   1 can condensed tomato
½ lb. processed cheese   soup and ½ cup milk
Salt   Buttered crumbs
Pepper

•   Cook macaroni according to directions on package. Cut cheese in pieces and melt over hot water in top of double boiler. Add liquid, stir until smooth and season to taste. Arrange in alternate layers with the drained macaroni in casserole. Top with buttered crumbs and bake in moderate oven (375°F.) until crumbs are lightly browned.

Yield: 6 servings. Note: 2 cups cream sauce may be combined with ½ lb. shredded American cheese and used with the macaroni. Slice stuffed olives or ripe olives may be mixed with the sauce. Noodles may replace the macaroni.

—From *Short-Cut Cook Book*, by Edith M. Barber. Copyright 1952. Published by Sterling Publishing Co., New York.

"YANKEE DOODLE" MACARONI
(6 generous servings)

2 medium-sized onions, chopped

2 sprigs parsley, minced

2 cloves garlic, minced (less if desired)

¾ cup sliced fresh mushrooms (or ½ cup canned mushrooms . . . 4 oz. can) (if desired)

3 tbsp. drippings (bacon, pork or beef, etc.)

1 lb. ground beef

3½ cups cooked tomatoes (1 No. 2½ can)

1 tbsp. salt

⅛ tsp. pepper

½ lb. macaroni (2 cups uncooked)

• Add onions, parsley, garlic and mushrooms to hot drippings in skillet, and cook until onions are a light golden color. Add the ground beef, and cook until brown. Add tomatoes, salt and pepper, and boil gently until thickened (about 45 minutes).

• Cook macaroni until tender (about 15 minutes) in 3 quarts boiling water to which 1 tbsp. salt has been added. Drain. Heap on hot serving platter.

• Pour hot tomato mixture over hot macaroni. Serve at once.

—From *Betty Crocker's Picture Cook Book* Copyright 1950. Published by General Mills Inc., Minneapolis.

BOILED MACARONI, NOODLES, OR SPAGHETTI
(Serves 6)

• Break macaroni (or spaghetti, or noodles) in 1- to 2-inch pieces or use whole. Drop into large amounts of rapidly boiling, salted water, using about 2 quarts water and 2 teaspoons salt for 1 cup macaroni. Boil 9 to 12 minutes, until tender. Drain and run cold water through it to prevent stickiness. Reheat with butter, buttered crumbs, Cheese Sauce, Tomato Sauce or any desired sauce. Eight-ounce package serves 3 to 4.

> —From *Fannie Engle's Cook Book* by Fannie Engle. Copyright 1946. Published by Duell, Sloan and Pearce, Inc., New York.

SCALLOPED MACARONI AND HAM

1 9-ounce package macaroni	2 tablespoons butter or margarine
½ cup bread crumbs	⅛ teaspoon pepper
1 cup chopped boiled ham	Milk
2 tablespoons minced onion	

• Cook macaroni as indicated in Boiled Macaroni recipe. Drain. Place half the macaroni in a buttered casserole, cover with half the ham, then with half the crumbs and onion. Dot with 1 tablespoon butter and add pinch of pepper. Repeat layers with remaining ingredients. Add milk, almost sufficient to cover. Bake in moderate oven (375°F.) for 20 to 25 minutes.

> —From *Fannie Engle's Cook Book* by Fannie Engle. Copyright 1946. Published by Duell, Sloan and Pearce, Inc., New York.

HAM-FILLED MACARONI RING
(About 6 servings)

¾ pound elbow macaroni
¼ cup melted butter or
  margarine
½ cup grated Parmesan
  cheese

2 tablespoons chopped
  parsley
Salt and pepper
¼ teaspoon Ac'cent

• Combine ingredients with macaroni (cooked until tender) mixing thoroughly.
• Pack mixture into well-buttered 5-cup ring mold. Set in shallow pan of hot water; bake in moderate oven (350°F.) until firm, 15 to 20 minutes. Unmold on heated platter.
• While macaroni ring is baking make a savory ham sauce as follows:.

2 slices bacon, diced
½ pound cubed, cooked
  ham
2 tablespoons each diced:
  onion
  celery
  green pepper

1 tablespoon flour
½ cup condensed tomato
  soup
¾ cup water
Salt
Pepper
Ac'cent

• Brown bacon in skillet; add ham and vegetables; brown lightly.
• Stir in flour until well mixed; add tomato soup and water; stir well. Cover and simmer over low heat, about 15 minutes. Season to taste. Serve in center of macaroni ring.

—From *The Book of Good Neighbor Recipes* by Maxine Erickson and Joan M. Rock. Copyright 1952. Published by Bond Wheelwright Company, New York.

MACARONI MOUSSE
(Serves 6)

1½ cups scalded milk	1 sweet green pepper,
¼ cup melted butter	chopped fine
3 eggs well beaten	1 tablespoon chopped
1 pimiento chopped fine	onion
1 cup cooked elbow	½ tablespoon salt
macaroni	1 cup soft bread crumbs
	½ cup mild cheese cut fine

• Combine ingredients in order given, reserving ½ cup crumbs. Sprinkle top with reserved crumbs. Bake 40 minutes, in pan of hot water in moderate oven (350°F.). Add ½ cup mushrooms, cut in pieces, if desired.

—From *The New Fannie Farmer Boston Cooking-School Book* by Fannie Merritt Farmer. Copyright 1936. Published by Little, Brown and Company, Boston.

TURKEY MACARONI

• Make a sauce with ¼ cup each of flour and butter, 1 cup of turkey stock, 1 cup of cream, and ½ cup of white wine. Add 2 cups of cubed turkey, 1 cup of cubed ham, 1 cup of boiled chestnuts, and salt and pepper to taste. Cook over hot water until well blended.
• Using the same sauce, add 2 cups of diced turkey, 2 cups of cooked elbow macaroni, and ½ cup of ripe olives. Put in a baking dish, cover with buttered crumbs mixed with an equal amount of Parmesan cheese. Bake in a moderate oven, until the top is browned.

—From *The New Fannie Farmer Boston Cooking-School Book* by Fannie Merritt Farmer. Copyright 1936. Published by Little, Brown and Company, Boston.

MACARONI AND CHEESE

• Boil macaroni 10 minutes; strain, and put alternate layers of macaroni and cheese in buttered casserole. Use the old-fashioned American cheese and plenty of it, chopped. Fill dish about ¾ full of milk, beat a couple of eggs, pour on top, and bake for 45 minutes in a moderate oven (350°F.) the last few minutes with a hot flame to give a crisp, brown top.
• Serve with homemade dill pickles or tart salad (chopped tomatoes, lettuce, celery, and onions suggested).

—From *Cookbook for Men* by Lew Lehr. Copyright 1949. Published by Didier, New York.

AUNT ELLA'S MACARONI AND CHEESE

• Boil ½ pound of macaroni (1½ cups) for 20 minutes in salted water. Drain. Grate 1¼ cups of American cheese. Add ½ of the cheese to macaroni, with ½ cup of melted butter and ½ cup of cream. Toss lightly and season to taste with salt and freshly ground pepper. Pour into buttered baking dish, sprinkle the remainder of cheese over the top and dust with paprika. Add enough milk to come nearly to the top of the macaroni mixture. Bake in slow oven (300°F.) until brown on top. (Spaghetti may be used instead of macaroni.)

—From *Aunt Ella's Cook Book* by Marguerite Gilbert McCarthy. Copyright 1949. Published by Little, Brown and Company, Boston.

FAMILY-STYLE BAKED MACARONI AND CHEESE
(Serves 3)
Cooking time: about 35 minutes

1 cup macaroni (small size or broken into 2-inch pieces)

¼ pound American process cheese, or cheesefood

1 tablespoon finely chopped onion (optional)

1 tablespoon butter

1 teaspoon flour

⅛ teaspoon dry mustard

¼ teaspoon salt

1 cup milk

¼ cup fine cracker crumbs

1 tablespoon butter

Dash of paprika

• Cook the macaroni in 1 quart of boiling water (and 1 teaspoon salt) until a piece feels soft when pressed with a fork. Drain well. Rinse under running hot water and drain again.

• Heat and set the oven at 400°F. Rub a quart casserole with salad oil, butter or margarine. Cut cheese into slices and then into strips. Use a saucepan over low heat or the top of a double boiler over hot water to make a sauce this way. Melt butter, add onion and cook slightly. Stir in flour, mustard and salt. Remove from heat. Stir in half the milk. Return to heat and stir until mixture begins to thicken; then stir in remaining milk. Stir and cook about 5 minutes. Now add cheese and stir until it is melted. Don't overcook. Combine the cheese sauce and macaroni. Stir lightly to blend, but don't break up the macaroni. Pour into the casserole. Cover with the crumbs. Dot with butter and add a dash of paprika. Bake in a moderate oven for 20 minutes. If this must wait, turn oven low and pour on a quarter cup of thin cream so the macaroni will be swathed in plenty of sauce.

—From *Modern Homemaker's Cookbook* by Beth Bailey McLean. Copyright 1950. Published by Barrows and Company, New York.

BAKED MACARONI SIZZLING SQUARES
(Serves 8)

½ pound of elbow or other macaroni broken into about 1-inch pieces
½ cup butter or margarine
¼ cup sifted bread flour
1½ cups warm milk
1 teaspoon salt

½ pound sliced frankfurters, sautéed in butter for several minutes
¼ pound American cheese cut in ¼-inch cubes
Medium sized fresh tomatoes

• Cook macaroni in boiling water about 25 or 30 minutes until tender. Drain well; pour into a large bowl and add 1 teaspoon salt to the cooked macaroni, mixing thoroughly.
• Melt shortening; add sifted flour, then the warm milk a little at a time. Cook over low flame until thick—5 minutes —stirring constantly. Add 1 teaspoon salt to sauce toward end.

• Pour the hot sauce over macaroni; mix well. Last, fold in sliced sautéed frankfurters and American cheese cut in ¼-inch cubes. Pour into wax-lined square pan that measures about 8 x 8 x 2. Let stand in room temperature until cool; then place in refrigerator for 6 or 7 hours or until absolutely cold and firm to touch. About ½ hour before serving time, remove from pan; cut into 4 (or more) square portions; place on well greased baking sheet. Pour 1 tablespoon of the following cheese sauce over macaroni and place a thick slice of tomato over sauce; pour more sauce over tomato. Bake in a 400°F. oven about 25 to 30 minutes. If not brown after thirty minutes place under broiler for a few minutes. May be served for supper or luncheon.

Cheese Sauce for Macaroni Squares

• Melt 2 tablespoons butter or margarine; add 2 table-spoons sifted bread flour and then 1 cup warm milk a little at a time. Cook over moderate flame until thick and smooth, stirring constantly. Then add ½ teaspoon salt and 1 cup freshly grated American cheese (¼ pound). Continue to simmer until cheese is fully melted. This is enough sauce for the tops of 1 recipe and there will be some left over, which may be served separately. Serve these squares with a green vegetable and salad. If sauce is too thick to be served separately, thin down with more hot milk.

—From *School Cookbook* by Antoinette Pope. Copyright 1948. Published by The Macmillan Company, New York.

CALIFORNIA MACARONI AND CHEESE
(Serves 6)

½ lb. (8 oz.) elbow macaroni	½ cup California sherry wine
4 tbsps. butter or margarine	½ tsp. dry mustard
4 tbsps. flour	1 tsp. Worcestershire sauce
1½ cups milk	Salt and pepper to taste
2 cups (½ lb.) grated American or Cheddar cheese	½ cup buttered fine bread crumbs

• Cook macaroni in boiling salted water until tender; drain. Melt butter and stir in flour; add milk and cook, stirring constantly, until mixture is thickened and smooth. Add cheese and stir over low heat until melted. Blend in sherry and seasonings. Mix with macaroni; turn into a

greased casserole; top with buttered crumbs. Bake in a
moderate oven (350°F.) 30 minutes, or until brown.
• VARIATIONS: Add 1 cup crabmeat, shrimp or tuna and ¼
cup chopped green pepper. Or add ½ cup sliced stuffed
olives, ¼ cup chopped green pepper and 2 tbsps. minced
onion.

—Italian recipe

MACARONI, TUNA AND APPLE SALAD
(Serves 4-6)

1 8-oz. pkg. elbow
  macaroni
1 7-oz. can (1 cup) tuna
1½ cups diced peeled
  apples
½ cup mayonnaise or salad
  dressing

1 cup diced celery
½ teaspoon lemon juice
¼ teaspoon salt
romaine
2 tablespoons chopped
  parsley

• Cook and drain macaroni, according to directions. Chill.
Flake tuna; add apples, mayonnaise, celery, lemon juice
and salt. Mix with macaroni and chill. Arrange on bed
of crisp romaine; sprinkle with parsley.

—Italian recipe

BAKED MACARONI AND CHEESE
(Serves 4-6)

3½ cups milk
1 (8 oz.) pkg. macaroni
½ teaspoon salt

⅛ teaspoon pepper
½ lb. sharp American
  cheese

• Scald milk. Stir in raw macaroni and cover. Add the
seasonings. Grate and stir in the cheese. Transfer to a
buttered 1½ quart casserole. Bake 30 minutes in moderate

oven, 350°F. Stir gently from bottom after first 10 minutes baking time.

—Italian recipe

TUNA MACARONI DINNER
(Serves 4-6)

1 (8 oz.) pkg. 20% protein
macaroni
1 can marinara, mushroom
or ragú sauce
1 (1¼ oz.) jar grated
Parmesan cheese

2 cups scalded milk
1 (7 oz.) can tuna fish
¾ teaspoon salt
1 (1 lb.) can mixed
vegetables

• Oil a 2-quart casserole. Put in the raw macaroni. Stir in the milk and cover. Drain the oil from the tuna and flake the fish. Add to the macaroni. Stir in the salt, sauce, liquid from the canned vegetables and the cheese. Cover and bake 10 minutes in a hot oven, 450°F. Add the canned vegetables. Stir gently from the bottom. Reduce the heat to 375°F. and bake 15-20 minutes longer.

—Italian recipe

TOMATO SAUSAGE CASSEROLE

1 (8 oz.) pkg. 20% protein
macaroni
1 can marinara, mushroom
or ragú sauce
1 teaspoon salt

3 cups hot water
1 (1¼ oz.) jar grated
Parmesan cheese
¾ lb. sausage meat

• Put raw macaroni, salt and half the cheese into an oiled 2-quart casserole. Add the hot water and sauce. Mix well. Cover; bake 15 minutes in hot oven, 450°F. Stir gently from bottom after first 10 minutes. While the

macaroni is baking form the sausage meat into 12 flat
cakes and brown well on both sides. Arrange on top of
baked macaroni. Bake uncovered 15 minutes longer.

—Italian recipe

MEAT LOAF
(Serves 4-6)

1 (8 oz.) pkg. 20% protein
elbow macaroni
1 can marinara, mushroom
or ragú sauce
1 (1¼ oz.) jar grated
Parmesan cheese
1½ cups milk

½ tablespoon grated onion
1½ teaspoons salt
1 teaspoon poultry
seasoning
1 lb. chopped raw beef or
equal parts beef, pork
and veal

• Scald the milk. Pour over the raw macaroni. Stir in
onion, salt, poultry seasoning and cheese. Add the sauce
and meat. Work with a spoon until ingredients are well
mixed. Oil an 8″ x 5″ loaf pan. Pack in meat mixture.
Bake 45-50 minutes in moderate oven, 375°F. to 400°F.

—Italian recipe

SCALLOPED CHICKEN
(Serves 6)

2½ cups milk
1 can condensed mushroom
  soup
1 8-oz. pkg. macaroni twists
½ lb. mushrooms
2 tbsp. butter
½ tsp. salt

Few grains pepper
2 cups diced, cooked
  chicken
1 cup buttered soft bread
  crumbs
2 tbsp. grated Parmesan
  cheese

• Combine milk and mushroom soup; bring to boil. Add uncooked macaroni twists; cover; let stand while preparing rest of ingredients. Slice mushrooms; sauté in butter; add with salt, pepper and chicken to macaroni mixture. Mix well. Pour into greased 2½-quart casserole. Toss crumbs and cheese; sprinkle on top of casserole. Bake in moderately hot oven, 375°F., 45 minutes.

—Italian recipe

CHEF'S MACARONI
(Serves 4-6)

1 8-oz. pkg. 20% protein
  elbow spaghetti
1 cup ham (or tongue)
  strips
1 cup chicken strips
½ cup cheese strips (Swiss
  or any piquant cheese)

Mayonnaise or Russian
  dressing
½ teaspoon salt
Dash pepper
Lettuce cups

• Cook macaroni according to directions, drain and chill. Combine with other ingredients and serve in lettuce cups.

—Italian recipe

ELBOWS A LA LUCERNE
(Serves 6-8)

1 8-ounce package elbow macaroni	¾ lb. chopped ham
½ pint sour cream	4 eggs, separated
	salt

• Cook and drain elbows according to directions. Beat egg yolks and add sour cream, salt and chopped ham. Combine with the elbows. Add stiffly-beaten egg whites to the mixture.
• Butter casserole pan and sprinkle flour on its bottom and sides. Add the elbow mixture and bake for 30 minutes in a moderate oven (325°F.).

—Adapted by Mme. Dora Dieu.

SEAFOOD PARTY RING
(Serves 6)

1 envelope plain gelatine	2 tablespoons mayonnaise
½ cup cold milk	2 tablespoons lemon juice
1½ cups scalded milk	⅓ teaspoon pepper
2 egg yolks, lightly beaten	1 can lobster (or shrimp,
1 teaspoon salt	crabmeat, tuna, etc.)
1 pkg. 20% protein elbow macaroni	

• Stir gelatine into the half cup cold milk. Turn into the scalded milk; add egg yolks and salt and cook gently in top of double boiler, stirring constantly until mixture coats spoon.

• Chill until just slightly jelled.

• Meanwhile, cook the macaroni in salted water according

to package directions. Chill by running cold water over macaroni. Drain thoroughly. Combine with mayonnaise, lemon juice and pepper. Mix in the flaked seafood.
• Finally combine with gelatine mixture and turn into ring mold. Chill until firm. Turn out onto platter and garnish with olive rounds and parsley.

—Italian recipe

MACARONI FRUIT FIESTA
(Serves 6)

½ lb. 20% protein shells
¾ cup diced raw pineapple
¾ cup pitted sweet
   cherries
¾ cup whole fresh
   strawberries

2 sliced bananas
¾ cup white grapes
½ cup fresh blueberries

Sour cream dressing to taste.

• Cook macaroni according to package directions. Drain and chill. Mix with dressing. Combine with fruit.

—Italian recipe

RIGATONI AND LASAGNE

STUFFED RIGATONI

1 (2½ oz.) jar grated
  Parmesan cheese
1 pkg. Rigatoni
Filling—Blend together:
½ lb. ground beef
¼ lb. ground pork
1 beaten egg
3 tablespoons grated
  Parmesan cheese
3 tablespoons bread crumbs
  or cracker meal

filling—continued
salt, pepper and chopped
  parsley to taste
½ can marinara, mushroom
  or ragú sauce
Sauce—Combine:
1½ cans marinara, mush-
  room, or ragú sauce
1 cup of milk
1 cup of water
1 teaspoon salt

• Hold Rigatoni like a cookie cutter, hole side down and plunge them into meat filling. The meat mixture will thus be forced up to fill the hollow Rigatoni. Cover bottom of deep casserole with sauce mixture. Add a layer of stuffed Rigatoni; cover with sauce mixture; add a generous sprinkle of Parmesan cheese. Repeat the process until all stuffed Rigatoni and sauce are in the casserole. Sprinkle cheese on top. Cover and bake in 400°F. oven for 50 min.
• Any desired filling may be used in place of the one suggested above; seasoned cottage cheese, sausage meat, chicken, leftovers, etc.

—Italian recipe

CREAMY LASAGNE
(Serves 8-10)

• One of the great traditional dishes of Italy is lasagne, a casserole made of the widest kind of ribbon pasta with many layers of sauce, several kinds of cheese, chopped

meats or meatballs. Recipes in the old cookbooks take up a page or two. And the doing is even longer than you might suppose. That's why there is so much excitement about the quick-frozen lasagne. Just as it comes, heated according to package directions, it makes a fine dish, but placed on top of a thick layer of cottage cheese...the dish becomes creamier and also less expensive per portion.
• You will need:

Marinara sauce	Grated pure Parmesan
Creamed cottage cheese	cheese
Chopped parsley	3 or 4 packages frozen
	lasagne

• Rub a shallow baking dish of the type that can come to the table, with a cut clove of garlic, and brush with olive oil.
• Cover the bottom of the dish with marinara sauce, then spread a layer of creamed cottage cheese about an inch thick. On top of the cheese place 3 or 4 packages of quick frozen lasagne. Sprinkle generously with grated Parmesan cheese.
• At serving time: Bring to the table in its own baking dish. Cut into squares. Pass grated cheese and chopped parsley.

—Italian recipe

SALADS

MACARONI SALAD
(Serves 8)

1½ lb. shell macaroni   1½ cups French dressing
4 sliced garlic cloves

• Cook macaroni in boiling salted water 20 minutes. Drain
in colander. Place cloth over colander. Place in oven to
steam dry. Place in bowl. Add garlic (which is speared
with toothpicks) and dressing. Toss until well mixed.
Chill at least 6 hours, or overnight; remove garlic. Add
juice of 1 lemon. Then add as many of following ingredients
as you like: 1 can shrimp diced, 1 cucumber shredded, un-
peeled and drained, 3 cups diced celery, 1 cup ripe olives
sliced, ½ cup green pepper shredded, 3 hard-boiled eggs
sliced, shredded carrots, cooked peas, sliced radishes un-
peeled, anchovies, any cooked vegetable or sea food. Add
mayonnaise and mix thoroughly.

> —From *Here's How; A Journey Through*
> *Good Food* by Helen Pendleton Rock-
> well. Copyright 1950. Published by Roy,
> New York.

CAPRI SEA SHELL SALAD
(Serves 6-8)

1 8-ounce package shells   3 cups crabmeat
1 cup diced celery   ½ cup capers
1 pkg. gelatin   salt and pepper
½ cup mayonnaise

• Cook shells according to directions and drain. Add the
crabmeat, celery, capers and seasoning. Soften gelatin in

½ cup cold water, add 1 cup hot water and the mayonnaise and combine with all other ingredients. Place in mold. When set, unmold and serve on lettuce leaves, garnished with olives and pimiento.

• VARIATIONS: 1. Instead of a gelatin salad, combine the ingredients with the mayonnaise and serve over a bed of watercress.

2. This recipe is delicious with other types of seafood as well—tunafish, shrimp, lobster, etc.

—Originated by Marie Angelin White, Nutrition Consultant.

CRAB MACARONI SALAD
(Serves 6-8)

1 8-oz. pkg. elbow macaroni
1 cup crabmeat
½ cup mayonnaise or salad dressing
¼ teaspoon oregano
1 cup cooked or canned peas
1 cup diced celery
¼ cup chopped onion
Lettuce

• Cook and drain macaroni, according to directions. Chill. Combine crabmeat, mayonnaise and oregano; mix well. Combine macaroni, peas, celery and onion; add crabmeat mixture. Mix well. Chill. Serve on bed of crisp lettuce.

—Italian recipe

SHELL SALMON SALAD
(Serves 4-6)

1 cup cooked shells
½ lb. can salmon, flaked
½ cup cooked or canned peas
½ cup diced celery
2 tablespoons chopped sweet pickles
1 tablespoon chopped onion

1 hard cooked egg
½ teaspoon salt
Few grains pepper
6 tablespoons mayonnaise or salad dressing
Lettuce
Sliced cucumbers
Watercress

• Chill shells. Combine shells, salmon, peas, celery, pickles, onion, salt, pepper and mayonnaise. Chill. Serve on bed of crisp lettuce garnished with sliced egg, cucumber and watercress.

—Italian recipe

ELBOW MACARONI—VEGETABLE SALAD
(Serves 4-6)

½ 8-oz. pkg. elbow macaroni
½ cup mayonnaise or salad dressing
2 teaspoons grated onion
¼ teaspoon marjoram
1 teaspoon salt
Few grains pepper
1 hard-boiled egg
2 tablespoons ketchup

Few grains paprika
½ cup diced celery
1 cup grated carrot
⅓ cup diced peeled cucumber
¼ cup chopped green pepper
watercress
Tomato wedges

• Cook and drain macaroni, according to directions. Chill. Mix together remaining ingredients except egg, tomato and watercress. Serve on crisp bed of watercress; garnish with egg and tomato wedges.

—Italian recipe

SEAFOOD SALAD
(Serves 6-8)

1 pkg. spaghettini
3 cups crabmeat, shrimp,
  lobster, tuna, or salmon
1 cup diced celery
Watercress
Pimiento

½ cup capers
Russian dressing or
  mayonnaise
½ teaspoon salt
Dash pepper
Olives

• Break spaghettini and cook according to directions. Drain and chill. Combine all ingredients except watercress, pimiento and olives. Serve on bed of watercress, garnished with pimiento and olives.

—Italian recipe

VEGETABLE SALAD
(Serves 4-6)

1 pkg. macaroni
1 cup cooked or canned
  peas
1 cup shredded raw carrot
½ cup diced celery
½ cup diced cheddar
  cheese
½ teaspoon salt
3 tablespoons chopped
  sweet pickle

3 tablespoons diced green
  pepper
2 tablespoons diced onion
Mayonnaise or French
  dressing
Dash pepper
Garnish: 3 hard cooked
  eggs, parsley, escarole,
  paprika

• Cook macaroni according to directions. Drain and chill. Combine all ingredients. Heap on escarole and garnish with quartered eggs, parsley and paprika.

—Italian recipe

SHELL SALAD
(Serves 6)

1 package shells or elbows
1 can of peas well drained
  or equivalent—fresh or
  frozen peas

1 small can of diced carrots
  or equivalent—fresh
  shredded carrots
1 cup of finely sliced
  celery

• Cook shells or elbows in well salted water until done; drain and cool slightly. Mix all of above ingredients in large bowl. Add salt and pepper to taste and add four to six tablespoons of mayonnaise or salad dressing.
• Can be served on a head of lettuce with garnishing of hard-cooked eggs.

—Italian recipe

DESSERT

MACARONI-RAISIN PUDDING
(Serves 6-8)

4 cups milk
1½ cups macaroni
½ cup seedless raisins
½ teaspoon nutmeg

2 eggs
½ teaspoon salt
½ cup sugar or honey

• Scald the milk. Mix in the raw macaroni, raisins and nutmeg. Transfer to a buttered 2-quart casserole. Cover and bake 10 minutes in a hot oven, 400°F. and stir gently from the bottom. Bake 10 minutes longer. Then beat the eggs light with the salt, and sugar or honey. Stir into the pudding. Cover and bake about 15 minutes longer at 350°F., or until firm on top. Serve warm with light cream.

—Italian recipe

Spaghetti from Bleecker Street to Park Avenue

When, early in 1953 Giovanni Buitoni was a sponsor of the Duchess of Windsor's ball for the benefit of the hospitalized veteran's music service—a highlight of the New York social season—one of the dishes served was a "crown of spaghetti with mushrooms." It is reproduced here with the note that it marks the passage of spaghetti from Bleecker Street to Park Avenue: a veritable milestone in the Americanization of spaghetti.

CROWN OF SPAGHETTI WITH MUSHROOMS
(Serves 4-5)

8 ounces spaghetti in "twists"	1 teaspoon heavy cream
1 teaspoon butter	1 egg, beaten
1 teaspoon flour	¼ cup grated Parmesan cheese
½ cup milk	Salt, pepper and nutmeg

• Cook spaghetti according to directions on package and drain.

• While it is cooking, make the sauce. Melt butter, blend in flour, add milk and cream, and cook, stirring, until thickened.

• Add egg, cheese and seasonings to taste.

• Add to cooked spaghetti and turn into a greased ring mold. Set mold in a pan of hot water and bake in a moderate oven (350 degrees F.) until set, about twenty minutes. While it is baking, prepare mushroom filling.

• To serve, unmold and place mushroom filling in center.

Mushroom filling:

½ pound fresh mushrooms, sliced
1 tablespoon minced shallots or onion
½ cup dry white wine
¼ cup butter
2 tablespoons flour
1 tablespoon lemon juice
¼ cup heavy cream
1 egg yolk, slightly beaten
Salt and pepper.

• Cook mushrooms and shallots or onion in wine, covered for fifteen minutes. Drain, reserving mushrooms.
• Cream together butter and flour. Add to wine and cook, stirring, until thickened. If necessary, add additional wine to thin sauce.
• Add lemon juice, cream, egg yolk and reserved mushrooms. Cook, stirring until thickened. Do not boil. Season to taste.

—Waldorf-Astoria recipe

Index

GIUSEPPE PREZZOLINI

COACHWHIP PUBLICATIONS

CoachwhipBooks.com

Pennsylvania German Cookery

A REGIONAL COOKBOOK BY
ANN HARK & PRESTON A. BARBA

COACHWHIP PUBLICATIONS

CoachwhipBooks.com

Blue Hills
and
Shoofly Pie

in Pennsylvania Dutchland

ANN HARK

COACHWHIP PUBLICATIONS

COACHWHIPBOOKS.COM

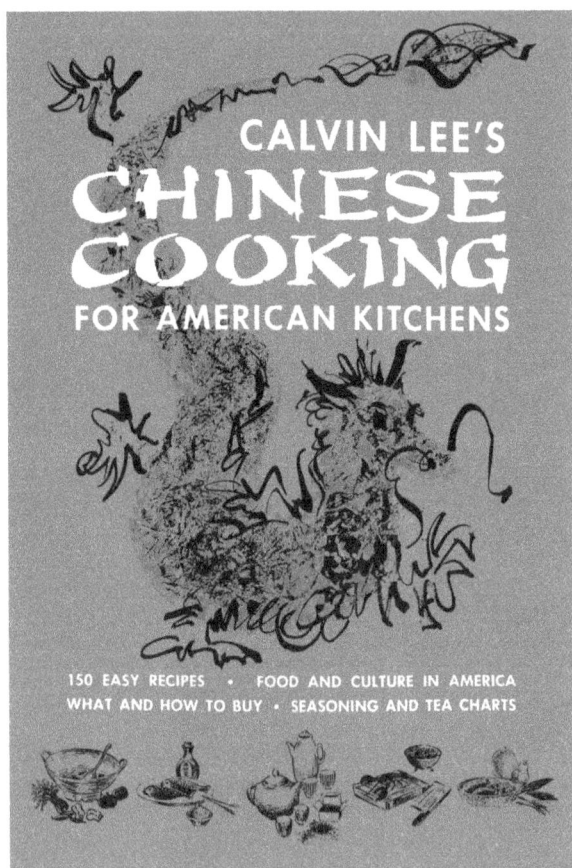

CALVIN LEE'S

CHINESE COOKING

FOR AMERICAN KITCHENS

150 EASY RECIPES · FOOD AND CULTURE IN AMERICA
WHAT AND HOW TO BUY · SEASONING AND TEA CHARTS

COACHWHIP PUBLICATIONS
CoachwhipBooks.com

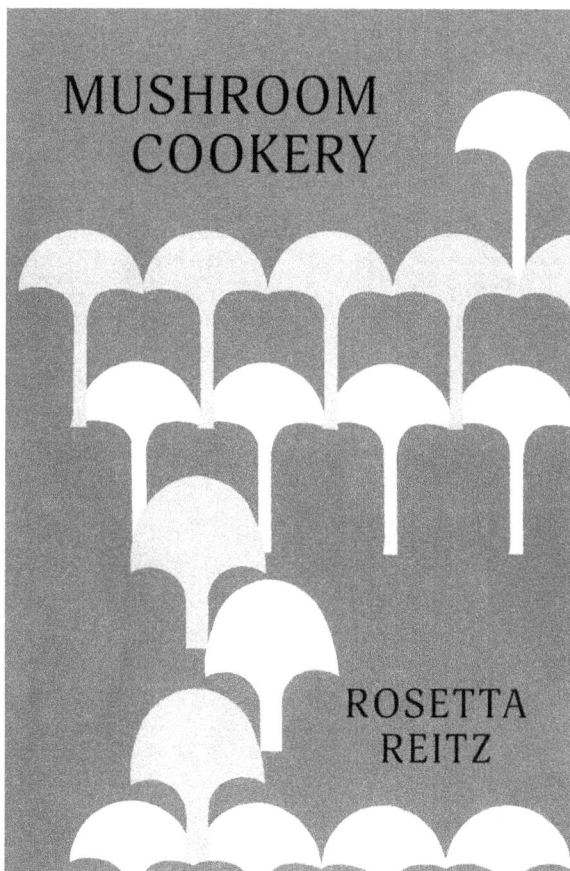

MUSHROOM
COOKERY

ROSETTA
REITZ

COACHWHIP PUBLICATIONS
CoachwhipBooks.com

AMERICAN INDIAN
COOKLORE

SYLVESTER AND ALICE TINKER | MAE ABBOTT | FLORA L. BAILEY

COACHWHIP PUBLICATIONS
CoachwhipBooks.com

Cherokee Cooklore

TO MAKE MY BREAD

Recipes

Herbs

Wild Foods

History

The Feast

Cherokee, North Carolina

www.ingramcontent.com/pod-product-compliance
Lightning Source LLC
LaVergne TN
LVHW091218080426
835509LV00009B/1061